TWAYNE'S WORLD AUTHORS SERIES

A Survey of the World's Literature

ARGENTINA

Luis Davila, Indiana University

EDITOR

Alfonsina Storni

TWAS 519

Alfonsina Storni

ALFONSINA STORNI

By SONIA JONES

Dalhousie University

TWAYNE PUBLISHERS

A DIVISION OF G. K. HALL & CO., BOSTON

Printed on permanent durable acid-free paper and bound in the
United States of America

First Printing

Library of Congress Cataloging in Publication Data

Jones, Sonia.
Alfonsina Storni.

(Twayne's world authors series ; TWAS 519 : Argentina)
Bibliography: p. 143–47
Includes index.
1. Storni, Alfonsina, 1892–1938—Criticism and interpretation.
PQ7797.S74Z665   861   78–15520
ISBN 0–8057–6360–0

For Gordon

Contents

About the Author

Sonia Jones was born and raised in London, England. She received her B. A. degree from Bennington College in Vermont, her M.A. from the University of California at Berkeley, and her Ph.D. from Harvard. She has taught Spanish language and literature at a number of universities, including Harvard, Tufts, and the University of California at Berkeley and Davis. She is currently Chairman of the Department of Spanish at Dalhousie University in Nova Scotia. Her articles on Lope de Vega have appeared in *Renaissance and Reformation* and *Reflexión 2*, and articles on Alfonsina Storni have been published in the literary supplement of *La Prensa*. Her beginning Spanish textbook, *Spanish One* (Van Nostrand Reinhold) is now in its second edition, and has been adopted by over one hundred colleges and universities in the United States and Canada.

Preface

The poetry of Alfonsina Storni first caught my attention when I was thumbing through anthologies, looking for some clear, simple verses to include in a beginning Spanish textbook that I was preparing. Although I had become familiar with her work during my years as a graduate student, for some reason I had not been struck at that time by the clear-mindedness she displayed in seeing through the sham and hypocrisy of social convention, or by the surprising courage with which she attacked many of the harmful traditions handed down over the years and unthinkingly accepted by the great majority of her compatriots. After reading her seven volumes of poetry, some of my initial impressions were confirmed. She was a lonely, passionate woman, sometimes overly sentimental and often narcissistic, but deeply loyal in her love and frustrated in her search for fulfillment. And yet, in spite of the fact that her poetry was very personal, the total picture of the poet herself still had many pieces missing. What caused her to think so hard and so long about human behavior and the frequently empty values of society? What experiences led her to reject what others confirmed, to think for herself, and to speak out so fearlessly? she lived at a time when women in Argentina were unquestionably in total subjection to husbands, fathers, and social regulations, yet she seemed to have broken away from the fetters that usually tied other women down. How did she succeed where so many had failed?

An examination of biographical and critical-analytical studies of her work was largely disappointing. Much of the material that dealt with her life was merely a compilation of anecdotes concerning the people she knew, the things she did, the places she visited, or the literary circles she joined. There were some fine and perceptive analyses of her poetry, but commentary about her inner life and motivations was almost entirely lacking. Even her friends, and many wrote about her, seemed not to know very much about who she really was. Various important aspects of her life, such as her relationship with her illegitimate son, were entirely overlooked or mentioned only in the most cursory way. There were also lacunae in other areas of obvious interest, the most noticeable one being the complete absence of critical analyses of her prose fiction and the extensive body of nonfictional prose. I was particularly intrigued by the occasional mention of a so-called feminist play she had written in 1927. Since it had closed in three days, critics through the years were of the unanimous opinion that the play was worthless, and it had long been out of print. But why had it failed? Was it really bad? had she offended some sector of the general public? My initial research in North America turned up other plays and a good number of essays and short stories that she had written, but the play that had failed was nowhere to be found. It was obvious that I would need to collect everything she ever wrote in order to assemble a more complete picture of the author. A trip to Argentina, for a number of reasons, was in order.

When I arrived in Buenos Aires, I soon realized that Alfonsina Storni was a national figure of considerable importance. There was a monument to her in Mar del Plata, where she had committed suicide, and all sorts of memorabilia had been collected by various enthusiasts. Most people knew her verses by heart, and one young woman even confessed that she kept an anthology of her poetry under her pillow. This is admittedly a rather unusual case of Alfonsina-worship, but it does serve to illustrate her enormous popularity. Yet this sort of public idolatry was something more than a little pernicious, for it emphasized the trivial and the sensational at the expense of the more permanent and valuable statements that Alfonsina had no doubt wished to express in her prolific writing. It was as if her well-meaning admirers had somehow locked her into a gilded cage made with the banners of their endless eulogies, covering her with flowers until the prisoner inside was finally hidden from sight. Alfonsina struggled all her life to free herself from the various cages that had threatened to hold her captive in one way or another, and she would have hated the idea of being finally trapped in one after her death. Perhaps this is the price of stardom, but it was clear to me that a reevaluation of her contribution to the literature of Argentina was overdue.

Several interviews with her son provided me with answers to some of the questions that had puzzled me, and her friends were able to shed further light on various aspects of her life and personality. But it was Alfonsina Storni herself who revealed to me what I was really looking for, and this is surely as it should be. I found the play that had attracted such negative criticism, and it was a veritable repository of her otherwise scattered opinions on women's rights, marriage, and human liberation. Her son gave me another play that had never been performed or published, as well as a few personal letters that had been exchanged between them just before her death. Weeks of work in archives and libraries produced the missing essays and articles that I had not been able to locate in the United States, and another short novel, long forgotten and out of print, turned up in a carton of papers belonging to one of her friends. When all these pieces were finally put together, there emerged a new picture of the author and her works which I have tried to portray as faithfully as possible in the present volume.

I have used Alfonsina's own essays throughout the book so that she could be permitted, whenever it was feasible, to speak for herself. Since I quote extensively from this material in every chapter, I have not set aside a special section to deal with her nonfictional prose, as I did in the case of her poetry and fiction. I have chosen to discuss her work generically, starting with her poetry, for which she is most widely known, and progressing to her plays, some of which have been reproduced and reprinted, and concluding with her prose fiction, most of which has been completely ignored. Within each genre, I have dealt with the material chronologically rather than thematically, for since the first chapter indexes the progressive development of her ideas, a chronological discussion within each genre makes it easier for the reader to compare her poetry, drama, and prose at various stages of her life.

Finally, I would like to express my deepest gratitude to the Canada Council for making it possible for me to conduct my research at Harvard University, the University of California at Berkeley, and in Argentina. I am also indebted to the Faculty of Graduate Studies at Dalhousie University for financing my initial foray to Harvard's Widener Library, and to the Interlibrary Loan Department of Dalhousie's Killam Library. I would like to thank Enrique Anderson Imbert, Professor of Romance Languages at Harvard, for introducing me to many helpful friends of his in Buenos Aires. I am particularly grateful to Alejandro Alfonso Storni, the son of the poet, for granting me so much of his time, and for letting me have a photocopy of the manuscript of his mother's unpublished play, *La técnica de Mister Dougall.* I would like especially to thank Fermín Estrella Gutiérrez, Vice-President of the Academia

Argentina de Letras, for orienting me so deftly when I first arrived in Buenos Aires, and for letting me have a copy of *Un alma elegante*, a short novel that was omitted from even the most complete bibliography of Alfonsina Storni's works. Many thanks are also due to the following critics, writers, and professors for providing me with sustenance, books, and information: Julieta Gómez Paz, Jorge Luis Borges, Victoria Ocampo, Roberto Giusti, Juan José de Urquiza, Blanca de la Vega, Juan Carlos Ghiano, Fryda Schultz de Mantovani, and María de Villarino. I would also like to thank Ramón Roggero, the editor of Alfonsina Storni's forthcoming *Obras completas en prosa*, for so generously letting me photocopy many pages of her articles which he had copied by hand from various sources that did not permit photoduplication. Many thanks to Antonio Negri for all his help and advice, and for presenting me with one of the few copies that still exist of the first edition of *El amo del mundo*. I am grateful to the following people for saving me endless hours of work by locating material for me: Señora de Etchepare, secretary to the President of the Academia Argentina de Letras; Señora de Negri, Director of the Archives at the Academia; Señora Mabel Hernández, Director of the Archives at the Sociedad Argentina de Escritores; Vicente Sierra, Director of the Biblioteca Nacional; Constancio Vigil, Editor-in-Chief of *Atlántida;* Enrique Mayochi, Director of the Archives of *La Nación;* Nereo Piaggio, Director of the Archives of *La Prensa*; and Patricio Peralta Ramos, Director of the Archives of *La Razón*. I shall always remember Mario Roza, publisher of Alfonsina Storni's *Poesías completas*, for introducing me to many helpful friends and for standing by me during the national strike. Finally, I would like to thank Luis Dávila, editor of the Twayne Latin American Authors Series, my colleagues Gustavo Alfaro and James Holloway, my friend Alicia Jurado, and my husband, for their careful reading of the manuscript and their very helpful suggestions.

SONIA JONES

Lunenburg, Nova Scotia

Chronology

1892   Born May 29 in Sala Capriasca, a town in the Italian sector of Switzerland. Daughter of Alfonso Storni and Paula Martignoni di Storni.

1896   Storni family returns to Argentina and settles in San Juan, where Alfonso and his brothers own a beer factory.

1897   Enters kindergarten in the *Escuela Normal*, San Juan.

1900   Storni parents and four children move to Rosario, where they open the Swiss Café.

1901   Enters the *Colegio de la Santa Unión* as a part-time student.

1904   The café fails; Alfonsina taken out of school to help her mother to support the family with her sewing.

1906   Her older sister marries, her father dies, older brother moves away, and she starts work in a hat factory to help support her family.

1907   Accepts first acting role in Manuel Cordero's company. Later goes on tour with another group under the direction of José Tallaví.

1908   Her mother marries Juan Perelli and moves to Bustinza. Alfonsina helps her give private lessons.

1909   Enters the *Escuela Normal Mixta de Maestros Rurales*, Coronda.

1910   Receives her title as "Maestra Rural."

1911   Begins teaching career in the *Escuela Elemental* No. 65, Rosario. Publishes first poems in *Mundo Rosarino* and *Monos y monadas*. Moves to Buenos Aires.

1912   Her son, Alejandro Alfonso, born April 21 in San Roque Hospital (now Ramos Mejía). Publishes first short story in *Fray Mocho*.

1913   Works as a shopgirl, and as a cashier in a pharmacy.

1914   Works as a market researcher for the import firm of Freixas Brothers.

1916   Publishes first collection of poetry: *La inquietud del rosal*. First woman in Argentina to join a literary circle; becomes member of "Nosotros." Begins to contribute regularly to *La Nota*.

1917   Receives the *Premio Anual del Consejo Nacional de Mujeres*. Begins teaching at the *Colegio Marcos Paz*.

1918   Publishes *El dulce daño*. Works at the *Escuela de Niños Débiles* in Chacabuco Park. Begins to write for the magazine *Atlántida*.

1919   Publishes *Irremediablemente*. Gives lecture at the University of Montevideo. Writes extensively for the magazine *La Nota*. Makes her first trip to Cordova to recuperate from nervous exhaustion. Publishes two short novels, *El alma elegante* and *La golondrina*.

1920   Publishes *Languidez*, which is awarded the *Primer Premio Municipal* and the *Segundo Premio Nacional de Literatura*. Becomes a regular contributor to the newspaper *La Nación*, sometimes using the pseudonym Tao Lao. Becomes a citizen of Argentina. Joins the literary group "Anaconda," headed by the novelist Horacio Quiroga.

1921   Begins teaching at the *Teatro Infantil Lavardén*. Writes first of many children's plays. Makes first trip to Mar del Plata.

1923   Teaches Drama and Speech in the *Escuela Normal de Lenguas Vivas*.

1925   Publishes *Ocre*. Organizes the *Primera Fiesta de la Poesía* in Mar del Plata.

1926   Publishes *Poemas de amor*. Teaches in the *Conservatorio de Música y Declamación* and in the *Escuela de Adultos Bolívar*. Joins the artistic circle "La Peña," headed by the painter Emilio Centurión and hosted by the Café Tortoni.

1927   Her first full-length play, *El amo del mundo*, opens on March 10 in the Cervantes Theater; closes three days later. Begins writing new play, *La técnica de Mister Dougall*.

1930   First trip to Europe, with Blanca de la Vega. Visits Italy, France, Switzerland and Spain.

1932   Publishes two full-length plays: *Dos farsas pirotécnicas*.

1934   Second trip to Europe, with her son Alejandro. Publishes *Mundo de siete pozos*. Joins the intellectual circle "El Signo."

1935   Undergoes radical mastectomy to remove breast cancer.

1937   Her friend Horacio Quiroga commits suicide.

1938   Gives another lecture at the University of Montevideo, with Gabriela Mistral and Juana de Ibarbourou. Leopoldo

Lugones kills himself. Quiroga's daughter also takes her life. Publishes *Mascarilla y trébol*. Suspects she has lung cancer. On October 25, in Mar del Plata, commits suicide by jumping into the sea.

CHAPTER 1

The Woman and Her Times

A LFONSINA Storni took great delight in playing the role of the
gadfly, relentlessly criticizing almost everything that fell
under her scrutiny, and never hesitating for a moment to express
her controversial opinions to anyone who cared to listen. Nor did
she lack the courage to live according to her own convictions, in
spite of a society unquestionably hostile to her unconventional behavior. She was an energetic, troubled woman who seemed to alter-
nate continually between powerful enthusiams and their attendant
disillusionments. She liked to read, but she had neither the time nor
the patience to be a truly dedicated scholar. What she expressed in
her extensive writing was learned mainly through her own experience and observations. It was inevitable, therefore, that her poetry
and fiction were a reflection of her dramatic, often painful, but
never uneventful life.

1 The Early Years

She was born on May 29, 1892,[1] in Sala Capriasca, a town in the
Italian sector of Switzerland.[2] Her parents were both of Italian Swiss
origin, but they had moved to Argentina in 1880, when her father,
Alfonso, began working with his older brothers in their beer factory
in the town of San Juan. The year before Alfonsina was born, Alfonso
and his wife, Paulina, decided to go to Switzerland with their two
older children to visit friends and family. They had planned to make
it a short visit, but they stayed several years. Alfonsina was four
when the family finally set sail again for San Juan, where the Storni
business was beginning to show signs of foundering.

Alfonso had long since grown tired of helping his brothers to run
the factory, but when it started to fail, he grew frankly discouraged.
He would take his dog and his rifle and disappear for days at a time,
sleeping outdoors and eating whatever he happened to find. The

young Alfonsina must have been impressed by this image of her
father the hunter, for a quarter of a century later she was to write a
sonnet in which she remembered him leaving at daybreak, followed
by his hound.

On the long road, just for something to do, he would stop and make his dog
cower by simply looking him straight in the eye. It would amuse him to split
open a snake's head with a single insolent bullet. He would stay away for
days on end, and like a hermit, he would eat birds and sleep on the bare
ground. "And only when the Zonda raises up great burning masses of sand
and insects in the hot deserts of San Juan, only then did he sing under the
skies."[3]

> De mi padre se cuenta que de caza partía,
> Cuando rayaba el alba, seguido de su galgo,
> Y en el largo camino, por divertirse en algo,
> Lo miraba a los ojos, y su perro gemía.
>
> Que andaba por las selvas buscando una serpiente
> Procaz, y al encontrarla, sobre la cola erguida,
> Al asalto dispuesta, de un balazo insolente
> Se gozaba en dejarle la cabeza partida.
>
> Que por días enteros, vagabundo y huraño,
> No volvía a casa, y, como un ermitaño,
> Se alimentaba de aves, dormía sobre el suelo.
>
> Y sólo cuando el Zonda, grandes masas ardientes
> De arenas y de insectos, levanta en los calientes
> Desiertos sanjuaninos, cantaba bajo el cielo.
>
> *Ocre (Ocher)*, 1925, p. 264

In spite of his daughter's good opinion of his marksmanship, he
would frequently return home from these hunting trips with nothing to show for his efforts but a mysterious hangover. Paulina
asked no questions. She sensed, perhaps, that if she put too much
pressure on him she ran the risk of driving him even further into his
own loneliness. His reactions to the failure of the beer factory had
taught her that he was a man who responded badly to stress, and
that he would do anything to escape from unpleasant tensions, no
matter what the cost. She noticed, too, that he was beginning to
drink far too much, so she did her best to make his life as serene as
possible, hoping that his interest in alcohol would eventually di-
minish. Her hopes were never realized. Alfonso continued to spend

his time hunting and drinking, while Paulina waited patiently for their lives to take a turn for the better.

Alfonsina, meanwhile, was thoughtfully observing her family, and very little escaped her notice. She realized that her mother was no longer receiving much financial or emotional support from her husband, and she was moved by the woman's suffering. By 1897 Paulina had already lost three of her children, one of whom died at birth, while the other two died a few months after their first birthdays. Alfonsina must have been deeply affected by her mother's sorrow, which she was to express years later in "Peso ancestral" ("The Heavy Weight of Ancestors"):

You said to me: my father did not weep. You said to me: my grandfather did not weep. The men of my race have never wept, they were made of steel. So saying, a tear dropped from your eye and landed in my mouth . . . I have never sipped poison so bitter from such a tiny goblet. Weak woman, poor woman who understands, I knew the pain of centuries when I drank it. Oh, my soul cannot bear its heavy burden.[4]

> Tú me dijiste: no lloró mi padre;
> tú me dijiste: no lloró mi abuelo;
> no han llorado los hombres de mi raza,
> eran de acero.
>
> Así diciendo te brotó una lágrima
> y me cayó en la boca . . . más veneno
> yo no he bebido nunca en otro vaso
> así pequeño.
>
> Débil mujer, pobre mujer que entiende,
> dolor de siglos conocí al beberlo:
> oh, el alma mía soportar no puede
> todo su peso.
>
> *Irremediablemente*, 1919, pp. 155–156

The last few years of the century were particularly difficult for the Storni family because they were losing the eminent position they had once enjoyed in San Juan society in the days when their business was flourishing. This position had been only grudgingly accorded them in the first place. Some of the small town people viewed them as upstart foreigners who had come to take advantage of them, so the Stornis' initial success aroused considerable anger and envy. Yet their precarious social position appeared not to bother the good-natured Paulina, who was genuinely friendly with everyone and who was delighted to see her neighbors imitate, in spite of themselves, her European clothes and customs. But when the beer factory began to fail and when Alfonso's misery became apparent, then the deeply rooted envy of the townsfolk was finally put to rest, and few people were able to disguise their pleasure at witnessing the downfall of the "outsiders." Paulina did not seem to lose her usual equanimity in the face of the small daily humiliations, but Alfonsina's adjustment was far less successful, for she had neither the experience to understand the fundamental unimportance of public opinion nor the temperament to bear the rebuffs and caustic comments without fighting back.

Her painful circumstances may have taught her to express herself in a way that was later to give her the reputation of being a writer with a sharp and acid wit. Certainly, however, she longed for the respect and approbation that was then being denied her and her family. Using her child's reasoning, it seemed to her that she could win the loving admiration of the people around her if only she could show them how precocious and clever she was. Accordingly, when she was still too young to know the alphabet, she sat on the front steps of her house, moving her lips and pretending to be deeply absorbed in reading a book which she held open on her knees, while at the same time anxiously watching out of the corner of her eye the dramatic effect she hoped to produce in the passersby. Long minutes passed and nothing happened at all, until some cousins of hers came along and began to laugh at her because she was holding the book upside down. Alfonsina ran into the house, weeping bitterly at her impressive failure to astonish the world.[5] Perhaps at that moment her destiny as a writer was settled, for she may very well have resolved then and there that she would find a way to capture the imagination and respect of her future readers. However that may be, there is no denying that she grew into a woman whose lifelong ambition was to express herself through artistic creation, while at the same time she retained the devilish urge to shock the bourgeois and to pull the beards of the self-important. This mischievous side of her comes out in "¿Qué diría?" ("What Would They Say?") a poem she was to include in one of her first collections, where

She wonders what the small-minded, empty-headed people would say if one bright day she were to give in to her wildest fantasies and dye her hair silver and violet, wear Greek shawls, change her hair-comb for a garland of flowers, sing in the streets to the tune of violins, and recite her verses in the public squares, free to say whatever she pleased. "Would they come out in droves on the sidewalks to see me?" she wonders. "Would they burn me at the stake as they burned witches? Would church bells ring to call them to Mass? The truth is, it makes me laugh just to think about it."

> ¿Qué diría la gente, recortada y vacía,
> Si en un día fortuito, por ultra fantasía,
> Me tiñera el cabello de plateado y violeta,
> Usara peplo griego, cambiara la peineta
> Por cintillo de flores: miositis o jazmines,
> Cantara por las calles al compás de violines,
> O dijera mis versos recorriendo las plazas
> Libertado mi gusto de vulgares mordazas?
> ¿Irían a mirarme cubriendo las aceras?
> ¿Me quemarían como quemaron hechiceras?
> ¿Campanas tocarían para llamar a misa?
>
> En verdad que pensarlo me da un poco de risa.
>   *El dulce daño* [*Sweet Pain*], 1918, p. 127

In spite of the various difficulties the Stornis had to endure in San Juan, Alfonsina's childhood there was certainly not one of relentless unhappiness. Because her parents were distracted by their own problems, she played by the hour with her older brother and sister, freely roaming the streets and doing more or less what she pleased. "I grew up like a little animal," she wrote, "without supervision, swimming in the canals of San Juan, climbing quince trees, sleeping with my head pillowed in grapes. Once when I was seven, I came home at ten o'clock at night, accompanied by the maid from a neighbor's house where I had gone after school, and where they had given me dinner."[6] The exceptional freedom she enjoyed in her San Juan days may partly account for the independent spirit that continued to manifest itself in everything she said and wrote for the rest of her life. But it is not difficult to imagine that the lack of parental guidance at this early age must have made her feel inwardly insecure and anxious for attention. "At eight, nine, and ten, I lie shamelessly," she went on to say. "I invent crimes, fires, robberies, that never appear in the police records. I am a bomb filled with hair-raising news; I am constantly embarrassed by my own tricks; I am trapped by them; I get my family into a mess; I invite my

teachers to spend their vacations on a ranch that does not exist . . .
the very exuberance of my lies saves me."[7] And the exuberance of
her imagination, one might add, was one of the cornerstones of what
was eventually to be her poetic creation.

II   *The Move to Rosario*

In 1900, when their fourth and youngest child was two years old,
the Storni family moved to Rosario. Alfonsina recounted this new
stage of her life in an interview thirty years later: "When I was ten
my father's fortune had been completely used up, and we left San
Juan so that our downfall would be less noticeable. And ever since
then, and I am not shy about saying this, I had to cope with life by
myself. Up until that time I was used to being waited on, but my
father was seriously ill, and my mother lacked the energy to take
care of the situation properly. If it interests you, I can tell you that I
worked with my hands—a decision I made on my own—and by the
time I was twelve I was earning the rent. I can assure you that I
earned it with the pride and joy that only a child my age, in the same
circumstances, could possibly understand."[8]

Life had indeed become difficult for the Stornis, who were by no
means accustomed to poverty. During their first year in Rosario,
Paulina gave private lessons to as many as fifty pupils, who paid her
just enough to keep the family going. Then, suddenly, Alfonso
awoke from his alcoholic dreams, and once more he became the man
of action who had appealed so much to his wife during their
courtship. He opened a café near the railroad station, and the six
Stornis installed themselves in the two back rooms. Paulina kept the
books and operated the cash register, the older children prepared
food and drinks, Alfonsina waited on tables and washed dishes,
while Alfonso, beer in hand, entertained the guests. The business
soon failed. Paulina, with Alfonsina's help, began supporting the
family by taking in sewing.

In 1906 many radical changes took place. Alfonsina's older sister
married, her older brother moved away, and, mercifully perhaps,
her father died. She now had even greater responsibility, for she
went to work in a hat factory where her salary, though pitiful, was at
least more than her mother earned from sewing. These difficult
years were of great importance in forming the unconventional
opinions that Alfonsina was later to express both in prose and verse,
for it was then that she learned to observe life from a viewpoint that

was not shared by other women writers, most of whom enjoyed the privileged life of the educated bourgeoisie. She later explained in an interview:

"You can understand that a person like me, who came in contact with life in such a direct way, in such a masculine way, let us say, could not live, suffer, or behave like a child protected by the four walls of her house. And my writing has inevitably reflected this, which is my personal truth: I have had to live as a man, so I demand to live by male standards. What experience has given me is greater than anything anyone ever told me. What I am doing is anticipating the woman of the future, because female standards all depend on the economic system. Our society is still based on the family, and the family rests on the authority of the man, who makes the rules. That is, he is the breadwinner and he decides what is to be done. But if the woman is the breadwinner, and she does not depend on any man, and if she can penetrate and overcome with her intelligence the legal network in which her system traps her, then she will automatically acquire men's rights, which to my mind are desirable because they are greater and based on higher standards than those of women."[9]

The following year Alfonsina had an experience that was to leave a strong impression on her future writing: she was allowed to have a role in a play performed by a company which had gone to Rosario on tour. She could hardly believe her good fortune. She had wanted to to be an actress for as long as she could remember, and for years she had pestered her mother, unsuccessfully, to let her set up a theater so that she could earn money for the family. Now at last she discovered for herself the excitement of rehearsals, costumes, performances, and applause. The local newspaper gave her a good review, as was to be expected, and she began walking on clouds. At last she had found an outlet for expression and a way to satisfy her need for approbation and acclaim. She was so successful in this first trial that another company soon invited her to become a permanent member of the troupe, and she spent the next year on tour with them. But one year was all she could take. In a letter to Julio Cejador she explained: "I was really only a child, but I looked like a woman, so life became unbearable for me. The atmosphere was choking me."[10] She was temperamentally unsuited for the stage, not only because she felt depressed by her life on the road, but also because she could not tolerate the emotional stress of acting. Years later a friend remarked that "she tired herself a great deal, and after every perfor-

mance she felt pressure on her chest. When she worked, very evident circulatory and respiratory changes took place. Even now
when she recites, although she has an inborn talent for acting, she
becomes overwrought and cannot control her emotions."[11] After her
year on tour she knew she could never become an actress, but the
experience was to help her write a good many plays over the course
of her lifetime.

III   *School in Coronda*

When she returned from her tour, she found that her mother had
remarried and moved to another town. She joined her there for a
few months, but soon realized that if she was ever to make something of herself, she would have to begin by going back to school. "I
decided to enter the first year [of teachers' training] in a normal
school that was just being opened," she wrote. "I had missed [the
equivalent of] the seventh, ninth, tenth, eleventh, and twelfth
grades. I went into the first year of teachers' training with a preparation I had acquired in three months, and I got my teaching diploma
with [the equivalent of] an A average."[12] The headmistress of the
school clarified matters many years later: "Her entrance exam was
not satisfactory, but it was necessary to be indulgent. The school had
just opened, and we needed students. Besides, we discovered in
Alfonsina a real desire to get ahead, to excel, to be something. She
studied eagerly; she read a great deal. She was sprightly, jovial,
communicative."[13]

Alfonsina was a tenacious, imaginative young woman, and no
doubt she acquitted herself well in the normal school, especially if
one takes into account her spotty academic background. One incident during her two years in Coronda, however, is worthy of mention, for it illustrates a theme that was to appear many times in her
poetry. Her colleagues at the school had noticed that she went to
Rosario every weekend, and this caused them to spend a good deal
of time speculating about the possible reasons for her mysterious
trips. Did she have a "special friend," or was she simply visiting
members of the immediate family? Nobody could guess, and there
the matter rested. When graduation day came, Alfonsina was once
more revelling in the enthusiastic applause of the audience who was
listening with evident delight as she recited her own poems and
sang popular songs. Suddenly a voice in the audience cried out that
this woman was a chorus girl who sang in a sleazy little theater in

Rosario. The voice was disdainful and accusing, Alfonsina was horrified because the accusation was true, the audience went sour, and a couple of catcalls were heard. That evening, when the landlady called her to supper, she found a note on her bed: "After what happened I do not have the courage to go on living."[14] The landlady and her husband rushed out to look for her, and finally discovered her sitting on a bench, staring at the river. When they approached her she stopped weeping, and within minutes she was her usual, cheerful self, joking and chatting as though nothing had happened. Her friends were always astonished to see how easily she could swing from a mood of profound depression to one of elation without any apparent transition. Her love of life, her yearning for death, and the peculiar ambivalence that these contrasting feelings aroused in her became a constant theme in her poetry. "Oh Death, I love thee, but I adore thee, Life," she wrote in "Melancolía."

She begs Life to let the spring sunlight shine on her one final time as she is being taken away in her coffin. She asks to be allowed to remain for a moment under the warmth of the sky so that the sun might penetrate her cold flesh. "I do not fear rest," says the last quatrain, "repose does me good. But first let me be kissed by the merciful wanderer who every morning, happy as a child, used to come to my windows."

> Oh, muerte, yo te amo, pero te adoro, vida . . .
> Cuando vaya en mi caja para siempre dormida,
> Haz que por vez postrera
> Penetre mis pupilas el sol de primavera.
>
> Déjame algún momento bajo el calor del cielo,
> Deja que el sol fecundo se estremezca en mi hielo . . .
> Era tan bueno el astro que en la aurora salía
> A decirme: buen día.
>
> No me asusta el descanso, hace bien el reposo,
> Pero antes que me bese el viajero piadoso
> Que todas las mañanas,
> Alegre como un niño, llegaba a mis ventanas.
>
> *Irremediablemente . . .* , 1919, p. 148

IV   *Unmarried Mother*

Alfonsina's first teaching position turned out to be in Rosario, so back she went in 1911 to assume her new duties. There she met and fell in love with a married man whom Conrado Nalé Roxlo describes as "an interesting person of certain standing in the community. He was active in politics—he became a provincial deputy—he was a journalist, and he had literary interests. Although he was of a Bohemian and disorderly temperament, he was undoubtedly a good man, and there was no deception. Alfonsina knew that there was a legal impediment to their union, but she loved him ardently, and she was not the calculating sort."[15] She was just nineteen when she discovered that she was pregnant. Probably the only thing she found disturbing about the news was the realization that she would have to leave her lover, for she knew perfectly well that if she were to stay in Rosario, she would have to put up with the insufferable abuse of the tightly closed provincial mentalities that surrounded her. She knew, too, that people would stop at nothing to ascertain who the father was, and she did not want to subject him to such an inquisition. "Who is the one I love? You will never know," she wrote in her collection of poetry in prose. "You will look into my eyes to find out and you will see only the radiance of my ecstasy. I will close him up within me so that you will never imagine who it is in my heart, and I will keep him there, silently, hour by hour, day by day, year by year. I will give you my songs, but I will not give you his name. He lives within me like a corpse in a grave, all mine, far from curiosity, indifference, and malice."[16]

With courage and sorrow, therefore, she resigned her post at the end of the school year and set out for Buenos Aires where she could live in relative anonymity. There she worked as a salesclerk in a pharmacy, later as a cashier in a store, and finally she found a reasonably decent job as a sort of market research analyst.[17] By the time she secured that position, she had already given birth to her son, Alejandro, a fact that she kept carefully hidden so as not to lose her post, for she was well aware that if her employers had known about her illegitimate child, they would certainly have been embarrassed by her presence on the staff.

This attitude on the part of her employers was evidently shared by her biographers, for they have all remained discreetly but rigorously silent on the subject of her motherhood. Clearly this silence was meant to be a token of their respect, but Alfonsina would not have wanted respect on those terms. She herself remained quiet about the topic only because she wanted to protect her son, her lover, and herself from malicious gossip, and because she knew that she had very little hope of being understood except by her closest friends. But motherhood is undeniably one of the most extraordinary events in a woman's life, and this important aspect of Alfonsina's biography should not be kept hidden. A careful examination of her lesser-known works, particularly her plays and articles, reveals a surprising amount of information about her opinions on love, marriage, motherhood, illegitimacy, women's rights, and many other related subjects. Her point of view on these matters is best expressed in an all-but-forgotten play called *El amo del mundo (The Master of the World)*.[18] Here the female lead, who also has an illegitimate son, turns down her suitor's condescending offer to forgive her for her unfortunate mistake. "One day," she retorts, "I shall tell you in detail, if it interests you, how it all happened. But not so that you will forgive me. I don't want to be forgiven. I was not just a little girl who was deceived. I did it on purpose, it was my own decision, I did it of my own free will, as a free person. Why should I want to be forgiven?"[19]

Nobody will ever know whether Alfonsina herself shared the beliefs of the character she created, but there is a strong possibility that her pregnancy was no mistake. She was a passionate young woman, headstrong and fearless, able to give herself completely to a love that meant everything to her. Yet it will always be hard to ascertain whether she formed her unconventional opinions because she needed to defend an action that branded her as a "fallen woman," or whether she lived from the very beginning according to a different code, a code understood and approved by very few.

The fact remains, however, that the opinions expressed in this play were fifty years ahead of their time. "Nice" women did not behave according to their own personal convictions, and not many women even voiced such ideas in Alfonsina's time. It is true that there were a few pamphlets circulated by the Argentine Anarchists in the 1920s, in which one could find some articles with advanced ideas about sexual freedom, but they were almost certainly written by men using women's pseudonyms.[20] What is more, the Anarchist pamphlets took a radical and unsubtle position on the question of "free love," often making the common mistake of confusing freedom with license. As far as can be determined, Alfonsina avoided that particular trap,which is why she was a truly original woman. She not only thought for herself, which was an accomplishment for a woman in her day, but she drew logical conclusions from her own observations and acted according to what she believed was right. One of her most unconventional conclusions dealt with the subject of marriage, an institution which had failed, she felt, largely because it was so terribly abused and misunderstood. The unmarried mother in *El amo del mundo* voiced the author's position very well when she declared: "I would never have made him [the father of her son] my husband. My passion and the truth in my heart were too strong. I loved a man for himself alone, without worrying about his intelligence, his social status, his background, or his education. I loved him innocently, without thinking about myself, and I threw all caution to the winds. That is the only way an honest woman can justify having a lover. But a husband, on the other hand, can be justified in all kinds of ways. Financial need, the fear of loneliness, a desire for companionship . . .Bah! Dozens of things."[21]

There was a fundamental honesty in Alfonsina that never permitted her to exploit the various advantages a husband can offer to superficial or unscrupulous women. It would be hard to believe that she never had any opportunities to get married; in all probability she simply preferred not to give up her freedom for the indignity of playing the role of a submissive child. Once when she was asked point-blank why she never married, she replied: "I realize perfectly well that one woman alone can never fulfill a man's ideal. This certainty would take all the illusion out of my marriage."[22] This was no doubt a polite way of saying that no man could possibly fulfill her own ideals. In an article entitled "The Male,"[23] she states that many men complain about the modern woman, who is no longer the docile, subservient creature she once was. But no woman can possibly be expected to subject her personality, which after all is the most valuable and intimate part of her being, to a man who is anything less than ideal. Since an ideal man would never make such a demand, Alfonsina innocently wonders whether there may be something slightly wrong with modern man's interpretation of what a woman's place should be.

Innocent questions can be laughed off and forgotten, but it was not so easy for society to ignore an unmarried mother who was obviously challenging its hallowed dicta by her act of unrepentant rebellion. Alfonsina thought it strange indeed that her critics were sometimes mothers themselves. "Mothers," she wrote, "whose special condition ought to soften their hearts and help them to understand that every woman who is in charge of another life is by definition a companion to them in pain, worry, and anxiety, have difficulty forgiving the so-called illegal mother, and their lack of charity contributes to the sacrifice of a reputation or of a young life."[24]

Fortunately the young life in question was not sacrificed. Her son, Alejandro, noticed very little hostility or hidden disapproval in the attitude of the people he knew.[25] He was popular at school, he excelled at sports, and his congenial personality won him many friends. His best friend, however, was Alfonsina herself, for he sensed how much she needed his understanding and support. He remembers his mother as a solicitous and affectionate woman who taught him to be independent from the start. She had developed a warm relationship with him which inspired his confidence and respect, and he, in turn, became a close and surprisingly mature companion to her at an early age. When Alejandro reminisces about this admirable relationship, one is especially struck by his mother's very earnest desire to teach him to understand the values she had learned to accept only after considerable suffering. More than anything else, she wanted her son to judge things for himself and to accept people on their own terms. It is a tribute to her strength and sincerity that she did not hesitate to encourage him to adopt the unconventional attitudes that had caused her to undergo so many difficulties in her own life. It would never have occurred to her to compromise with the truth as she saw it. She felt a certain pride in her solitary struggle against society, as witnessed by one of her early poems, "La loba" ("The She-Wolf"):

"I am like a she-wolf," she claims. "I broke away from the pack and went to the mountains, for I was tired of the plains." In this poem she is very proud of her son, "the fruit of love, of a lawless love," for she could not be like the others, living like oxen with yokes on their necks. Like the she-wolf, she roams alone and laughs at the flock. She finds her own food and is completely self-sufficient, for she knows how to work and her mind is sound. She invites anyone who shares her courage to follow her in her wanderings, but she warns them that it is a difficult life, although she fears nothing and is always ready to face any challenge, whatever it may be. "First my son, then me, and then . . . come what may!"

Yo soy como la loba.
Quebré con el rebaño
y me fui a la montaña
Fatigada del llano.

Yo tengo un hijo fruto del amor, de amor sin ley,
Que yo no pude ser como las otras, casta de buey

Con yugo al cuello; libre se eleve mi cabeza!
Yo quiero con mis manos apartar la maleza.
. . . .
Yo soy como la loba. Ando sola y me río
Del rebaño. El sustento me lo gano y es mío
Donde quiera que sea, que yo tengo una mano
Que sabe trabajar y un cerebro que es sano.

La que pueda seguirme que se venga conmigo
Pero yo estoy de pie, de frente al enemigo,
La vida, y no temo su arrebato fatal
Porque tengo en la mano siempre pronto un puñal.

El hijo y después yo y después . . . ¡lo que sea!
Aquello que me llame más pronto a la pelea.
A veces la ilusión de un capullo de amor
Que yo sé malograr antes que se haga flor.

Yo soy como la loba.
Quebré con el rebaño
y me fui a la montaña
Fatigada del llano.

La inquietud del rosal (Disquietude of the Rosebush),
1916, pp. 59–60

V *The Role of the Sexes*

"La loba" is a poem that reveals quite a different side of Alfonsina's character, one which predominated when she was still a very young woman during her early years in Buenos Aires. Her initial reaction to the stinging commentary that she must have heard was to fight back in the only way she knew how: with witty insolence, an aggressive sense of superiority, and a few well-chosen words which were calculated to offend the "inferior minds" who had attacked her. While it is true that she never got over her feeling of outrage whenever she encountered a typical Babbitt whose ideas were conveniently packed away in cubbyholes, she nevertheless learned to temper her once violent reactions to mediocrity and maliciousness by developing a gently ironic, albeit sometimes acid, sense of humor. Poems like "La loba," however, were the kind that her readers tended to remember best, for they attracted a great deal of negative attention by their tone of unabashed defiance. Even such an intelligent critic as González Lanuza was so put off by her choice of themes that he went so far as to assert that she had failed as a poet because she was never able to transcend her own problems. "In her best poems," he writes, "there appears with fatal regularity an element of aesthetic impurity, an inorganic residue not properly assimilated, a prosaic quality which festers and takes the vitality from her verses. This is not meant to be a reproach . . . perhaps it can be explained if we keep in mind that Alfonsina began to write in a hostile atmosphere, bristling with obstacles for any woman with intellectual pretensions. Her sex was a drawback. Even though she had spirit, the difficulties she encountered must have been enormous. Because she was an intelligent and pugnacious writer, the danger would later acquire some rather subtle dimensions. She accepted the challenge, and this was both her greatest merit and her irreparable mistake. Her merit lay in the fact that she dared to demand the rights that were being denied her; her mistake was trying to be a poet, because poetry cannot serve anything but its own ends. Least of all can it serve as an escape-valve for personal resentments; and in every poem of Alfonsina's first stage there appears, hardly repressed at all, an expression of her resentment of men and an obsession with the eternal masculine."[26]

González Lanuza's comments are debatable, for in the course of literary history one can find very few themes, if any, that have not inspired poetry. It seems self-evident that the poet, and not the theme, is responsible for the poetic creation. González Lanuza's words are pertinent to this section, however, because they are a typical example of the way many critics misunderstood Alfonsina, whom they accused of writing nothing more than embittered soapbox harangues in verse. In order to make his argument convincing, González had to limit his criticism to just one small portion of the total picture. In the first place, he was speaking only of her early poetry and some of her less successful stories. Even Alfonsina herself lamented the fact that she had allowed these youthful poems to be published at all: "That book [*La inquietud del rosal*] should have been burned, but it is a common mistake for people here to launch an immature book just because the author seems promising, when in fact our literature would stand much to gain if every promising author were required to submit himself to some rigorous discipline before being introduced to the public."[27] In the second place, González Lanuza, like many other critics, placed too much emphasis on what he understood to be her resentment of men. When Edmundo Guibourg, a person whom she respected a great deal, also joined the others in complaining about her attitude toward men, she became thoroughly exasperated. "Oh, Guibourg, Guibourg! I have spent my entire life praising men," she wrote. "Three hundred love poems, Guibourg, three hundred, and all dedicated to the beautiful, reasoning animal! Why did you not thank me before, in long articles of adulation, just as you are now upbraiding me because, according to you, I abused one, just one, a single case, whereas I keep on adoring the rest, always ready to die for the magnificent enemy?"[28]

Alfonsina did not resent men. We should believe her when she said that she was always ready to die for the magnificent enemy. But what she wanted to do was to make him into an enemy for whom it was worth dying. She knew that the first step was to cure him of the false idea he had of his own superiority, a superiority which allowed him to look at a woman as though she were nothing. What is worse, he took it upon himself to fix the rules of the game, and Alfonsina wasted no time in chastising him for expecting her to live by a double standard.

In one of her best-known poems, "Tú me quieres blanca" ("You Want Me to be Pure"), she asks with sarcastic innocence why her man can come to her, his lips reddened with fruit and honey, and expect her to be chaste. She tells him to wipe his lips and go to the woods, live in a cabin, touch the damp earth with his hands, sustain himself with bitter roots, sleep on the frost, toughen his body with salt and water, talk to the birds, and set sail at dawn. When at last he becomes hardier and manages to extricate his soul from other bedrooms, only then can he expect her to be white, pure, and chaste.

> Tú que hubiste todas
> Las copas a mano,
> De frutas y mieles
> Los labios morados.
> . . . .
>
> No sé todavía
> Por cuales milagros
> Me pretendes blanca
> (Dios te lo perdone),
> Me pretendes casta
> (Dios te lo perdone),
> Me pretendes alba!
>
> Huye hacia los bosques;
> Vete a la montaña;

Límpiate la boca;
Vive en las cabañas;
Toca con las manos
La tierra mojada;
Alimenta el cuerpo
Con raíz amarga;
Bebe de las rocas;
Duerme sobre escarcha;
Renueva tejidos
Con salitre y agua;
Habla con los pájaros
Y lévate al alba.
Y cuando las carnes
Te sean tornadas,
Y cuando hayas puesto
En ellas el alma
Que por las alcobas
Se quedó enredada,
Entonces, buen hombre,
Preténdeme blanca,
Preténdeme nívea,
Preténdeme casta.

El dulce daño (Sweet Pain), 1918, pp. 120–121

Alfonsina was quite right to feel annoyed at so often being un-justly accused of resenting men. If she criticized them, it was only to point out to them the error of their ways, in the hope that any improvement would lead to a much-needed rapprochement be-tween the sexes. She understood quite well that men and women alike would have to struggle hard to rid themselves of the false values that insinuate themselves so silently into every life. This struggle would be as hard for women as it was for men, but mean-while the former were clearly the victims. She declared once in an interview: "My greatest failure has been not to be able to convince those around me that, since I have a masculine brain, I have the right to live my life with the independence, the dignity, and the decorum with which any normal man can live his."[29] In spite of her understandable impatience, Alfonsina had a strong sense of justice because even though the great majority of men did not know how to appreciate her "masculine" brain, she was always willing to admit that men, in the last analysis, were just as intelligent as women.

VI *A True Feminist*

By the time the first World War broke out, Argentina had made almost no progress at all in establishing civil rights for women. While suffragettes were causing an uproar in Europe and North America, women in South America were still being callously exploited. Not only were they being outrageously underpaid for working long hours, but many employers interfered in their personal lives as well. The telephone company, for example, would not allow its female employees to marry, thus contributing to the existence of illicit unions and illegitimate children. Women in Argentina were making slow progress compared to women in other parts of the world, but it was progress all the same. One by one, doors to formerly all-male professions were being reluctantly opened to them. Alfonsina pointed out, in one of her sardonic essays on the subject, that although Buenos Aires had recently welcomed into its labor force the first lady furniture refinisher, she sincerely doubted that any men would ever demean themselves by clamoring to join a woman's profession. It would be a long time, she surmised, before seamstresses would have to fear any competition from men.[30]

Alfonsina herself constituted a notable first when she managed to pry open the door to one of the local artists' and writers' associations, which had previously been firmly closed to all women. Roberto Giusti, who was later to become a close friend of hers, recalls the occasion: "Alfonsina Storni made her first appearance in our intellectual circles back in 1916, when she published *La inquietud del rosal* . . .Ever since that night in May this congenial little schoolteacher, who was then just a vague promise, a hope that became necessary to us at a time when women who wrote poetry— very few—generally belonged to a subspecies of literature, was a faithful comrade to us in our gatherings, and little by little, imperceptibly, the intellectual esteem we had for her began to grow, until one day we realized that we had in our midst an authentic poet."[31] It must have occurred to her that if she had been a man, she would probably not have had to wait so long for others to become aware of her talent, but she was satisfied to have broken new ground and to have been accepted by those who shared her intellectual interests. Her new contacts gave her a fresh impetus and undoubtedly boosted her self-confidence. The years that followed turned out to be among the most productive in her life. In 1918 she secured a teaching position which gave her a bit more time for herself, and she began to publish her poetry at the rate of one volume a year: *El dulce daño (Sweet Pain)*, 1918; *Irremediablemente (Irremediably)*, 1919; and *Languidez (Languor)*, 1920. She also contributed articles to a large number of journals and newspapers, among them *La Nota*, *Nosotros*, and *La Nación*.

Many of these articles dealt with the subject of women's rights. Alfonsina was perfectly aware of the obvious fact that women could never hope to achieve any sort of self-respect and independence unless they were allowed to participate fully in the workaday world, on an equal footing with men. What made her articles original, however, was her ability to see beyond the day when women would finally accomplish their goals. She was never content, for example, merely to point out how ridiculous it was for women to be banned from the polls. She knew that women would eventually get the vote (this was not to come about, however, until thirty years later), but what interested her was what would happen to them when they succeeded.[32] She wrote:

One of these fine days you are going to be shocked by an extraordinary piece of news: you will be given the right to vote. You will be transformed overnight into a citizen. Does that not give you gooseflesh? A citizen! does that word not evoke the beautiful days of ancient Greece when the citizens would gather to deliberate in the squares; or the Roman Assemblies, during which the voters would cast their tablets, giving the name of their candidate? . . . Have you thought about the weighty responsibility which is going to fall on you now, you who have done nothing more so far than bring four or five children into the world? . . . Then you have probably succumbed to your major defect: taking things too seriously. You are no doubt impregnated with idealism and with various heroic misconceptions which may have even led you to believe that there is great truth in what the books say about Greece, Rome, the French Revolution, and human equality. . . . [During pre-election campaigns] you will see a man speaking from a podium, you will hear his words, and you will want to be guided by them right into the depths of his soul, just as lightning is led by the lightning rod. You will hope to find in him a great sense of responsibility, but your high expectations will be smashed against an artificial world of deceit, tricks, lies, and self-interest.[33]

Alfonsina has sometimes been criticized for not being more socially and politically involved. Although she dedicated some of her writing to social criticism, she never joined any activist groups or participated in political movements. This is probably because she perceived the futility of any attempt to establish social reform if it is not first preceded by reform on the individual level. She knew that women would never be liberated simply by winning the right to enter a world of dishonesty and corruption. What she hoped to achieve through her critical essays was to raise the consciousness of all individuals, both men and women, in order to make them more clearly aware of the various human weaknesses and failings that are at the root of the social evils she so deplored. Mere protest would not have been enough for her. She was interested in seeking the causes of the injustice she saw, and the possible solution, she believed, lay in elevating the moral standards of the individual. She dedicated much of her writing, therefore, to analyzing the false values by which so many people lived, and she was certainly not above poking fun at anyone whom she felt deserved to be chastised.

Those who took the greatest exception to her sometimes ruthless satire were invariably men, no doubt because they were unused to being criticized so openly by the "inferior" sex. Many women, too, adopted a disapproving attitude toward her unseemly behavior and bold statements, but it was the men, in their function as critics and journalists, who managed to get their opinions into print. Although many of them expressed admiration for both her verse and prose, there were plenty of others who persisted in blinding themselves to the fundamental purpose of her work, preferring instead to present to their readers the image of an embittered woman who wanted nothing more to do with men. Even Enrique Anderson Imbert, echoing González Lanuza's words,[34] writes: "She set her poetry alight with the embers of her resentment of the male sex, but she also injured it [her poetry] by giving it elements of aesthetic impurity . . . . Finally, in her struggle against men, Storni triumphs; but at the cost of her own sensitivity. She is like the plant which triumphs over the sap, and dries up. Is this a triumph?"[35] She may have been disillusioned with men, and she was often exasperated when treated as their inferior, knowing she was superior to many of them, but she never compromised her own humanity. Certainly it is time now to change this erroneous picture of her which has emerged as a composite of so many one-sided views.

Since the criticism published about her was written largely by men, it is not surprising that they should have concentrated on what

they termed her bitterness toward the male sex. It is not too surprising, either, that her critics should have totally overlooked a
major portion of her work: that which dealt with her relentless
denunciation of women. Time after time Alfonsina upbraided
women for being frivolous, calculating, superficial, hypocritical, narrow-minded, and lacking integrity, but nobody ever accused her of
being bitter or resentful toward the female sex. She had no patience
at all for the provincial mentality of small-town women, whose malicious gossip had victimized many a spirited young girl; [36] she mer-
cilessly satirized empty-headed women whose only goal in life was to
step out into the street looking irreproachably coiffed and mani-
cured; [37] and she chided flighty girls for spending all their energy
trying to track down a husband to relieve them of the responsibility
of thinking for themselves. [38] Nothing annoyed her more, however,
than the type of woman she called a "perfumed feminist," whom she
ungallantly compared to the duck-billed platypus [39] because she was
a hybrid between the old-school belle and the new, independent
woman. This female platypus, she complained, would approach the
editor of a newspaper, for example, and land a job as a staff reporter
by merely batting her eyelashes. She has probably never done anything in her life before other than polish her fingernails, but she
manages to skip the normal stages of apprenticeship because she has
used her feminine charms on her boss. The articles she writes are
deplorable, the other journalists are jealous of her quick promo-
tions, and she becomes a living example of the preconceived notion
that women have no talent or ability except as sex objects. So the
true feminists, Alfonsina concludes, who are struggling to win the
respect of the male world, once again suffer a setback at the hands of
unscrupulous women.

Although Alfonsina was not the first feminist in Argentina, she
may have been the first to understand the real meaning of feminism.
She knew that if women were to achieve their full spiritual and
intellectual potential, they would have to give up using their so-
called feminine wiles in their efforts to get ahead in a world created
by men for men. In 1920 she wrote: "It bothers me to be a woman
because through sheer common sense I have had to give up all my
old defenses, and yet I am left with the usual disadvantages of my
sex. Other women, however, are still making hypocrisy such a way
of life that they seem to be the normal ones, while I, by contrast,
look out of place."[40] She was no doubt exasperated by the tendency

among women to look for the quick and easy way to worldly success
by using hypocrisy and sex to achieve their goals. She knew, too,
that men were just as tempted to get what they wanted through
tricks and subterfuge, and she never tired of criticizing these practices. What she deplored most of all was the fact that such habits
inevitably carried over into people's personal lives, thus making it
impossible for men and women to enjoy with one another anything
but the most callous and superficial relationships.

As a true feminist, Alfonsina wanted to bring about nothing less
than a spiritual revolution, and naturally she was destined to fail. She
was asking men to give up their selfishness and their unfounded
feeling of superiority; she wanted women to stop being frivolous and
hypocritical; she hoped that both men and women would treat one
another as human beings, rather than continue in their pitiful game
of mutual exploitation. What she was saying was not very different
from the basic principles of many religions: know thyself, transcend
thy ego, love thy neighbor. If this can be accomplished, the rest falls
naturally into place. But of course it could not be accomplished, and
Alfonsina grew increasingly disillusioned. She had grasped a simple
and essential truth, she believed, and yet she was unable to communicate this truth to others in a way that would inspire them to feel
as she did. What was worse, they frankly misunderstood much of
what she was trying to express, and they angrily accused her of
being an embittered woman who was blaming men for her own
failures in life. A vicious circle was soon established because she,
too, reacted to their accusations with considerable bitterness. If she
is to be criticized in this regard, it is not because she showed hostility toward the male sex, but because she only went halfway in
practicing what she preached. She expected people to be able to
free themselves from the false and pedestrian claims of their egos,
but she herself never fully transcended her own ego because she
allowed herself to feel outraged at the personal criticism that was
leveled at her. One cannot help but sympathize, however, with the
angry impatience she felt toward her detractors who had so unjustly
accused her. She had an important message, she felt, and all she
wanted to do was tell others about it. Why did they insist on twisting
her words? Why could they not understand what she was trying to
say? Nobody could give her any answers to her exasperated questions.

Alfonsina herself ascribed it all to the fact that the people in
Buenos Aires were hopelessly bourgeois. "When I say 'bourgeois',"

she wrote, "I am talking about anyone who has not been uplifted by ideas, inspired by spiritual things, ennobled by great art."[41] This is a definition that fits the great majority of people everywhere, but Alfonsina believed that women were at a special disadvantage in that they had always received an artificial education which had taught them to be submissive, docile, and to avoid thinking for themselves. The brainless women who emerged from such a training were condemned from the start to be bourgeois. It was difficult for them to be uplifted by ideas if they were never permitted to read anything more stimulating than women's magazines; they were hardly likely to be inspired by spiritual things if they were expected to learn everything secondhand instead of by their own experience; and as for being ennobled by great art, it was obviously impossible for a woman without any preparation to appreciate an artistic masterpiece. It is not hard to imagine that Alfonsina felt suffocated in such an atmosphere. "I find that I am terribly out of place," she complained, "just as out of place as anyone else who lives according to ideas and feelings, especially if they are his own ideas and feelings. But even though this is difficult for a man, it is still much easier for him than it is for a woman."[42] She had learned from her own experiences that people were more likely to listen to a man. "When a woman has the temerity to say what she thinks, other women are alarmed to hear their own secret thoughts reflected in her words, right there in plain daylight."[43] She is no better off trying to communicate with a man, for "a woman who thinks and feels too much displeases men, who prefer to be believed without having to be subjected to extensive female questioning."[44] She had her difficulties even with the well-intentioned men who had accepted her into their intellectual circles, for at first they most probably listened to her with a benevolent courtesy that must have infuriated her. "There have been an infinite number of times when I felt deeply disturbed at being a woman, for although I have been able to forget that I am in the presence of men, they themselves have had great difficulty in forgetting that I am a woman."[45]

Perhaps if she had been able to take herself less seriously, she might have viewed her situation with more of a sense of humor. But it was no doubt hard for her to maintain a proper perspective when every situation she encountered in her life presented some sort of a challenge that had to be met and overcome. She was opening entirely new roads, and it was surely not easy for her to have to do it

alone. In spite of her sharp tongue, she could be a lively woman who
charmed others with her cordial laughter. But occasionally this
laughter would become too strident, as though she were hiding a
feeling of inner sadness. "Those who knew her superficially were
amazed at her jovial conversation and her brilliant *repartee*, which
emanated from her cheerful and restless spirit. In her intimate life,
however, she became very serious, almost hermetic."[46] There was
nothing for her to do but resign herself to the difficult role she had
chosen. She must have faced many moments of depression and
loneliness, but she never lost sight of the better world she envisioned, for with a prophetic voice she was able to proclaim, full of
hope and confidence: "The day will come when women will dare to
reveal how they really feel. That day our values will be turned
upside down, and fashions will surely change."[47]

VII   *Life as a Recognized Poet*

By the time she was twenty-eight, Alfonsina had won considerable recognition for her poetry. In 1920 her fourth book, *Languidez* (Languor), won not only the First Municipal Prize, but also
the Second National Prize, which at that time were very coveted
awards. The previous year she had been invited to give a series of
lectures at the University of Montevideo, where she spoke about
the woman whom she considered to be the greatest poet of Latin
America: Delmira Agustini. She felt a great affinity for Delmira,
whose passionate verses and tragic sense of life struck a responsive
chord in her. "I think Uruguayans should pay just homage to the
author of *Empty Chalices*," she said in an interview. "A plaque in
the cemetery seems such a small thing to me. What is needed is an
entire monument right in the middle of the city."[48] As a woman who
had endured many injustices in her own life, she must have
identified strongly with this poet whom she so greatly admired, for
Delmira had suffered the greatest injustice of all, that of being mur-
dered. Years later Alfonsina wrote a sonnet in which she described
the profound sympathy she felt for the unhappy woman who, long
since dead and buried, was unable to defend herself from the sen-
tentious, pompous, and boring words that were pronounced over
her tomb.[49]

Another outstanding woman poet, Juana de Ibarbourou, also at-
tended the lectures. Years later she recalled: "In 1920 [sic] Alfonsina
came to Montevideo for the first time. She was young and she

seemed gay; at least her conversation sparkled, sometimes witty, sometimes sarcastic. She inspired enormous admiration and sympathy. . . . She was lionized by a group of the most illustrious members of the intelligentsia and of Montevideo society, who crowded around her and followed her everywhere. Alfonsina, in that moment, must have felt a bit like a queen surrounded by her court."[50] Alfonsina was equally impressed with Montevideo, and her affectionate memories of the city were to constitute an important theme throughout the rest of her poetry.

But in spite of her success in gaining both recognition and a decent income, Alfonsina was succumbing more and more frequently to her bouts of depression. It is not unusual, of course, for people to feel unexpectedly let down at the very moment of achieving a hard-fought victory. She makes this point herself in one of her early poems, "La tristeza" (sadness): She describes how a feeling of sadness sets in when a difficult venture has been accomplished, for then one no longer has any illusions. The triumph has wiped out the goal which had once been the great moving force.

> Pero yo pensaría que nació la tristeza
> Después de aquel momento en que algo se logró.
> Cuando el triunfo de haber gustado la proeza
> No permite aún crear otra nueva ilusión . . .
>
> *La inquietud del rosal*, 1916, p. 45

Be that as it may, the circumstances of her life were undoubtedly pushing her to the brink of nervous exhaustion. Her lectures, travels, teaching, constant moves, and the frenetic pace of her publishing schedule were all taking their toll, not to mention the time and energy she spent caring for her small son. She felt so thoroughly worn out, in fact, that she became convinced that she had contracted tuberculosis. Her doctor did not agree with her self-diagnosis, but he did suggest that she take a long vacation. So she packed her bags and went to Cordova, where she was able to get the rest she needed. This was to be the first of many trips to Cordova, and her son Alejandro remembers with special warmth those restful pauses in an otherwise hectic life.[51] Alfonsina, too, found peaceful satisfaction in contemplating the beautiful surroundings. A new tone of serenity began to appear in *Ocre (Ocher)*, a collection of her poetry which was published in 1925. She was to remember in "Un recuerdo" ("a Memory"):

those pleasant moments in the mountains of Cordova, where she wandered
among the wild mint, her soul emptied of all desire, while day after dazzling
day passed by with no surprises.

> Recuerdo el dulce tiempo de sierras cordobesas
> Pasado con el alma sin un solo deseo,
> Vagando entre las matas de menta y de poleo,
> Los cielos deslumbrantes, los días sin sorpresas.
>
> *Ocre,* 1925, p. 268

In 1921 her friend Roberto Giusti managed to secure for her a
special position teaching drama in the Children's Theater of Lavarden. Alfonsina threw herself into her new work with her usual enthusiasm. She had a great rapport with children, and this made it
easy for her to establish with them a kind of spontaneous and unin-
hibited relationship which helped to make them feel at ease on the
stage. The children grew to love her, and they performed well. But
Alfonsina soon felt dissatisfied with the stilted and unimaginative
children's plays that were being used at the school, so she began to
write material of her own. She knew what appealed to children,
what made them laugh, what frightened them, and what held them
spellbound. Her students were excited about their new roles, and
Alfonsina directed the performances with greater energy than ever,
delighted, no doubt, to be able to use her own material and her own
music. She and the young actors in her charge began to draw the
crowds when they performed in the public parks and squares of
Buenos Aires, but in spite of their not inconsiderable success, her
plays for children never appeared in print until Ramón Roggero
collected and published them in 1950.[52]

Alfonsina had been interested in the theater ever since her earliest childhood, but her years with the Children's Theater of Lavarden gave her the impetus she needed to sit down and actually write
plays. In 1927 she wrote her first full-length play, *El amo del
mundo.* Since she was known to the public primarily as a poet, her
new role as playwright attracted substantial attention. "What
prompted you to seek new modes of self-expression in the theater?"
she was asked in an interview the day before opening night. [53] "I
have been intending to write for the theater for some time," she
replied, "because this is the kind of prose which best accommodates
itself to my essential laziness. I like to read and write short material,
so I feel tempted and excited by the theatrical mode because it

synthesizes." Later in the same interview she was asked what kind of plays she planned to write in the future. "I am fascinated by plays that depict unconventional people who let their personal conflicts reach the maximum pressure-point. They represent a certain type of person in today's world. I would like my characters to reflect such a person, multiplied by an infinite number of variations. There is no doubt in my mind that I shall give preference to studying the complexities of women, with all their weaknesses and courage, even though I know ahead of time that I shall be criticized for making my male characters a mere backdrop for the female leads." Her prediction proved to be partly correct, but she was also criticized for putting the male protagonist of *El amo del mundo* in an unfavorable light, and the play closed after only three days. She was infuriated but not discouraged by the criticism, for in the four years that followed she wrote three more full-length plays and another play for children. [54]

All during the 1920s and 1930s, Alfonsina maintained a close and continual contact with the artists and intellectuals in Buenos Aires. One of her most intimate friends was the Uruguayan novelist and short-story writer Horacio Quiroga, who was the central figure of a group that called itself the "Anaconda," after Quiroga's novel of the same name. They would all get together for discussions in obscure restaurants and cafés that had not yet been discovered by tourists and Philistines, or they would gather in Quiroga's house where the ample garden, overrun with weeds, housed an astonishing menagerie of jungle animals, including a monkey, a coati, an anteater, and various species of snakes and birds. Alfonsina was in her glory when she was joking and gossiping with her friends, reciting her poetry to them, listening to their opinions on the latest books, or scribbling witty epigrams on the spur of the moment to be read aloud for the amusement of the group. Members of the various literary circles had a genuine interest in hearing or seeing the creations of their colleagues, and a good deal of mutual criticism was exchanged. Some of the groups developed a particular artistic philosophy of their own which they loved to debate with members of some opposing group, as in the case of the famous Boedo and Florida circles, but Alfonsina was not a joiner in that sense. She never associated herself with any one point of view, preferring instead to come to her own conclusions and express herself in her own way. She demonstrated an unfailing enthusiasm for literary gatherings, however. She personally organized the first Festival of Poetry at the seaside resort of Mar del Plata, and she became a devoted habituée of "La Peña," a distinguished artistic circle organized by the painter Emilio Centurión, and hosted by the Café Tortoni. One might go so far as to say, without too much exaggeration perhaps, that her love for the literary life was every bit as great as her dedication to literature itself.

In spite of all the good fellowship that Alfonsina enjoyed with her literary friends, she was still troubled by intermittent depressions. In 1928–1929 she took Alejandro out of school and went with him to Cordova, where she slowly recovered from a nervous breakdown. By 1930, however, she was ready for another vacation from the tensions of Buenos Aires, so when Blanca de la Vega, her close friend and colleague in the Conservatory of Music and Drama, suggested that she accompany her on a trip to Europe, Alfonsina accepted without a moment's hesitation. Her spirits lifted almost from the moment they set sail. [55] They went to Italy and France, and from there they made a quick side-trip to Switzerland, where they visited Sala Capriasca, the town in which she was born. She was deeply moved by this return to native soil, and she was delighted to talk to a number of people who remembered her as a girl.

They spent the following two months in Spain where they were well received by the intelligentsia. Jacinto Benavente was a particularly warm host, and they had memorable conversations with Ortega y Gasset, as well as with other outstanding writers and poets. Alfonsina was very disappointed, however, to discover that she and other Argentine literati were almost entirely unknown to the general public. Although some journalists were past masters at the art of writing highly laudatory articles that actually said nothing at all, [56] they betrayed their ignorance of her country by asking her whether Argentinians had ever heard of Russian ballet.[57] With her usual sense of fair play, Alfonsina was quick to admit that both countries suffered from a mutual lack of knowledge: "It is true that we are also guilty of harboring enormous misconceptions about Spain," she said in an interview. "Seville is a big city of about a million inhabitants, with every modern convenience and good hotels, like the Alfonso XIII, which is just splendid. It is not a city of mantillas and haircombs, it is something much more serious, with neighborhoods that are elegant and graceful. It represents Spain's smile, but not her laughter."[58]

While she was in Spain, Alfonsina did what she could to rectify these misconceptions by lecturing extensively and granting interviews to all and sundry. "She believes," wrote a journalist who spoke to her on her return to Argentina, "that the moment has come for us to send some well-informed people to Spain on a lecture tour to publicize the work of Argentine artists."[59] She herself made an effort to fulfill this need. "Right now I am trying to get a position as consul somewhere in Europe," she explained. "I would like to serve my country by making its culture better known abroad. I think that writers would make excellent consuls because they could reflect the social realities of the countries they represent through public lectures and newspaper articles."[60] In an ideal world she would have been a fine consul, but she was never given the opportunity to prove her ability in this area, no doubt because whoever was in charge of making consular appointments knew that the combustible, outspoken poet would have stepped on too many toes. Alfonsina also knew that it was unlikely that she would ever be named consul. Her failure to achieve this position becomes even more understandable in the light of what she said about herself and her social circumstances in an interview that took place several years previously: "My character lends itself poorly to adulation and petty political maneuvering, and in this sense I have always been my own worst enemy. I know perfectly well that I lack the necessary talent to live by social formalities, and it is not because I do not know how, but because the whole idea repels me. I have always lived, and I shall continue to live, like a feather in the breeze, with no shelter of any kind. This is very bad in an environment which judges everything by appearances. Here, when a person is being considered for some restful and important position, such as the kind that are given to writers so that they can dedicate themselves to their work, nobody asks whether that person is likely to produce something of value, but rather whether he is good at living according to social formalities. And when an individual has the frightful simplicity and audacious frankness to talk as I am doing now, he is immediately disqualified from that polite, starchy class of people who are so dear to officialdom."[61]

In 1934 Alfonsina went to Europe again, this time accompanied by her son Alejandro. When she returned, she published another collection of poems, *El mundo de siete pozos (The World of Seven Wells)*. In those years she spent many a night with a literary and

artistic circle called "El Signo," which used to meet in the Grill of
the Hotel Castelar. There the people "drank less coffee than they
did at 'La Peña,' but a good deal more whiskey, and often they
would dance until dawn."[62] The "Signo" group was considered very
Bohemian. The men often went so far as to appear tieless at public
events, at a time when it was unthinkable to dress without a tie on
such occasions. Alfonsina was absolutely in her element in this cordial and unconventional atmosphere. There she met Federico Gar-
cía Lorca, and she became a great admirer of Ramón Gómez de la
Serna, who gave some memorable talks to an enthusiastic crowd. In
the wee hours of the morning, when most of the people had gone
home, she would stand by the piano and sing tangos in a throaty,
vibrant voice, adding a touch of mischievous irony to her sexy imitations of professional singers. There is no question that Alfonsina was
experiencing the happiest times of her life with the "Signo," but
unfortunately, it was not to last long.

VIII   The final years

One day in 1935 when she was sitting partly in the water on the
beach in Mar del Plata, Alfonsina was startled to feel a sharp pain as
a wave hit her on the chest. When she examined herself she discovered quite a large lump in her right breast, and her first thought was
cancer. This time her self-diagnosis turned out to be correct, and on
May 20 of the same year, she underwent a radical mastectomy.
When she first saw the scars on her chest and arm she felt
thoroughly repelled, and for a time she succumbed to one of her
terrifying depressions. She would only allow her most intimate
friends to visit her in the hospital, and even after she was released,
she tried to live as much as possible in seclusion. Little by little she
began to drop her old friends altogether, for she found their unspoken knowledge of her illness and their tacit sympathy to be absolutely unbearable. She tried to forget that she had ever had cancer,
and the very word became taboo to her. She never referred to her
operation when she was in the company of her new acquaintances,
although she did speak occasionally of having been hospitalized for a
nervous breakdown.

During the years that followed she slowly pieced things together
again, and she approached her old friends once more with what
seemed to be her usual spirit. But, underneath it all, things were
never to be the same. When in 1937 her friend Horacio Quiroga,

who had been suffering from cancer of the prostate, committed suicide by drinking cyanide in the hospital, she wrote "A Horacio Quiroga," a poem that was to be prophetic.

It would be nice to die the way he did, the poem states, for then it is all over in a moment. She congratulates him for his courage, reminding him of the old saying that every hour wounds us a little, but the final hour is the one that kills us. Fear rots us more than death, so let others say what they will, he was right to drink the poison.

> Morir como tú, Horacio, en tus cabales,
> y así como siempre en tus cuentos, no está mal;
> un rayo a tiempo y se acabó la feria . . .
> Allá dirán.
>
> No se vive en la selva impunemente,
> ni cara al Paraná.
> Bien por tu mano firme, gran Horacio . . .
> Allá dirán.
>
> "Nos hiere cada hora—queda escrito—,
> nos mata la final."
> Unos minutos menos . . . ¿quién te acusa?
> Allá dirán.
>
> Más pudre el miedo, Horacio, que la muerte
> que a las espaldas va.
> Bebiste bien, que luego sonreías . . .
> Allá dirán.
>
> Sé que la mano obrera te estrecharon,
> mas no, sí, Alguno, o simplemente Pan,
> que no es de fuertes renegar su obra . . .
> [Más que tú mismo es fuerte quien dirá.][63]

In January of 1938 she was invited to give another lecture at the University of Montevideo, this time as a participant in a program that included talks by Gabriela Mistral and Juana de Ibarbourou. The three women were unquestionably the best-known women poets in Latin America, and the lecture hall was filled to capacity by an admiring audience, eager to hear what they had to say. Alfonsina's speech, entitled "Entre un par de maletas a medio abrir y la manecilla del reloj" ("Between a Couple of Half-open Suitcases and the Hands of the Clock")[64] because she had put it together hastily during her trip to Montevideo, is a valuable document providing many biographical details as well as personal opinions of her own work.

When she returned to Buenos Aires she was shocked to learn that Quiroga's daughter had also committed suicide. This news caused her to withdraw even further into herself, and she began to spend hour after hour alone, thinking and writing. Later that year she published her last collection of poems, *Mascarilla y trébol (Mask and Clover)*, which turned out to be a radical departure from her earlier work in both content and style. She was no longer interested in human passions; instead she preferred to dwell on themes that she considered to be of a more abstract, universal nature. Her poetry was now generally thought to be hermetic and obscure. She lost a considerable number of her readers, in addition to those who had already fallen away because of the unpopular themes of *El mundo de siete pozos (The World of Seven Wells)*, but she was not outwardly concerned. In this last year of her life she seemed to have finally found the courage to shrug at the opinions of her critics, but it would also appear that she had lost all interest in what had always inspired her the most: the study of human nature in all its multi-faceted complexity.

Since the time of her operation, her suffering had continued almost unabated. She had great pain in her right arm, she experienced terrible attacks of insomnia, not to mention the extraordinary anguish she felt when she suspected that the cancer had reappeared in a lung. This time she refused to see a doctor in spite of the urgent requests of her friends, who remembered only too well that she had threatened several times to kill herself if her illness recurred.[65] She even left Alejandro for the first time in her life and moved into an apartment alone, claiming that she was afraid that if she did have cancer in her lung, it might in some way be contagious. She probably did not have the heart to even think about suicide while her son was near her. She knew that their mutual love was the only force that could possibly stop her, so she moved away.

In October, 1938, she announced that she was going to Mar del Plata for a rest. Alejandro wanted to go with her to keep her company, but she would not even hear of it. She told him she needed to be left strictly alone in order to recover her strength, so he respected her wishes. There is probably no better testimony to the close and affectionate relationship enjoyed by mother and son than the last letters exchanged between them just before she took her own life. Alejandro shows great concern for her condition and gives her advice on how to care for herself. She, in turn, tries to reassure him that she is feeling better, but her letters are not very convincing. "At least I have been able to get some sleep," she writes in one of these unpublished letters. "I slept in the train all night. I am writing you this while reclining in my seat, and I do not have to support my hand. My appetite is better, but I still feel very weak. And my depressions! I am so frightened of them. But I must have confidence. If I recover my physical strength, maybe the rest will fall into place."[66]

On October 24 Alfonsina's arm hurt her so much that she had to dictate her letter to Alejandro to the maid. She begged her son to think about her, and she told him that she was only writing to him to let him know that she loved him. In this letter she called herself his sister, a term she had first used long ago to protect herself from being harassed for having an illegitimate child, and which had later come to symbolize their close relationship with each other. Later the same day she sent her son a final note in which she told him that she had had an attack of paralysis and that she could no longer go on living. Her words clearly indicated both her deep love for her son, and the despair which drove her to suicide. Shortly after writing this note, she struggled to the end of a pier in a raging storm in the middle of the night and threw herself into the smashing waves. The next morning some fisherman found her body washed up on the beach. The sky was blue from horizon to horizon, and her expression was serene.

Hours later the newspaper *La Nación* received a letter she had sent some days earlier, containing her last poem. In this sonnet, entitled "Voy a dormir" ("I Am Going to Sleep"), there is a tone of peace and resignation.

She personalizes the dewy grass and flowers of her burial place, and speaks to them as to a nurse who will gently put her to bed and cover her with sheets of soft, mossy earth. Her night light will be a constellation of stars, and she asks to be left alone, to rest in peace. "Oh, and if he telephones again," she says in the last tercet, "tell him not to insist, that I have gone out . . ."

Dientes de flores, cofia de rocío,
manos de hierbas, tú, nodriza fina

> tenme prestas las sábanas terrosas
> y el edredón de musgos escardados.
>
> Voy a dormir, nodriza mía, acuéstame.
> Ponme una lámpara a la cabecera;
> una constelación; la que te guste;
> todas son buenas; bájala un poquito.
>
> Déjame sola: oyes romper los brotes . . .
> te acuna un pie celeste desde arriba
> y un pájaro te traza unos compases
>
> para que olvides . . . Gracias. Ah, un encargo:
> si él llama nuevamente por teléfono
> le dices que no insista, que he salido . . .[67]

Alejandro had indeed telephoned her several times during those last days, for he felt unconvinced by her reassuring words. He was troubled by premonitions the whole time she was in Mar del Plata, so when he turned on the radio on the morning of October 25 in the middle of a news broadcast that was describing the tragic event, he did not have to wait to hear the name of the person involved—he knew then and there that his mother was dead.[68]

The newspapers were soon flooded with articles about her. The worst ones lavishly praised her work with flowery generalizations, or lamented her death with solemn words which were intended to be appropriate for the occasion. Alfonsina would have read many of the commentaries with disapproval. Earlier the same year she had written an article in homage to Leopoldo Lugones, who had also just committed suicide. "I have chosen everyday vocabulary," she wrote, "to express the pain I feel . . . and if I were not so reticent about using gilt-edged words, I would ask: why should the dead be locked up in a gilded cage? Their work lives on as their best testimony, far superior to any critical opinion. The greatest homage one can pay a writer is to refrain from burying his tragedy with bouquets of beautiful words. We should try, instead, to penetrate its meaning without being afraid to face the truth."[69] It is to her great credit that Alfonsina herself struggled all her life to accomplish just that.

CHAPTER 2

The Poet

ANY attempt to classify Alfonsina's poetry by applying to it the usual literary labels is bound to fail. This may very well be true of all poetry, but suffice it to say that, in Alfonsina's case, she never consciously allied herself with any particular literary philosophy. She was interested in studying the goals put forward by the various artistic schools both inside and outside Argentina, but her approach was eclectic. Her early work reflects a predominantly Romantic tone, with its autobiographical elements, its lyrical and sometimes sentimental themes, and its overall tendency to portray the sensitive, rebellious, misunderstood poet standing alone against the world. Yet even in her first volume there is considerable influence from the Hispanic Modernist movement, which developed primarily as a reaction against the worn-out imagery of Romanticism. The Modernists never entirely succeeded in disassociating themselves from their predecessors, however, for they still clung to the old desire to withdraw from prosaic reality into an idealized world of their own invention. The longing for a better world has been described, of course, in the poetry of all ages. But the Modernist dream differed from the Romantic ideal of noble savages in a pastoral setting in that it depicted, instead, the essentially Parnassian vision of an exotic, artificial universe. Alfonsina is using Modernist imagery in "Lo blanco" ("That Which is White"): when she likens a woman's alabaster hand to the silks of Japan and China, the veins to fine tulle, while at the same time she sees in this hand a symbol of infinite harmony and perfection.

> María, cuando tiendes tu mano marfilina
> Que asemaja la seda de Japón o de China
> Para cortar las flores de tus ricos jardines
> Me parece escuchar un rumor de violines.

51

Porque tus manos son armonía infinita,
Arte que se condensa en la forma bendita
De perfección, y tienen las venas tan azules
Que parecen bordadas en finísimos tules.
                              La inquietud del rosal, 1916, p. 29

One of the symbols which was used most frequently by the Modernists to depict the ideal of ephemeral beauty was the swan, first popularized by Rubén Darío and finally laid to rest in 1911 by Enrique González Martínez in his famous sonnet, "Tuércele el cuello al cisne" ("Wring the Swan's Neck").[1] Alfonsina, however, was still temporarily refusing to let the poor creature die, for five years later there he was again in "Los Cisnes" ("The Swans"), floating in the usual exotic setting, with his neck in its customary question-mark position:

Hecho un interrogante su cuello es como el símbolo
Del alma que encarnaron y allá van suavemente
Preguntando al Misterio el misterio insolvente

Y al verlos desfilar vuelto enigmas se piensa
En la leyenda blanca del extraño Lohengrin
Tirado por un cisne sobre el agua del Rhín.
                              La inquietud del rosal, 1916, p. 22

Alfonsina was criticized by many Modernists, however, for failing to write poetry whose primary goal was to create "art for art's sake." The critic Eduardo González Lanuza, himself a poet of Modernist tendencies at a certain period in his development, deplored the fact that she used her poetry as "an escape-valve for her personal resentments,"[2] for "Art is a difficult god to please. [That god] demands of those who would approach him a complete and absolute surrender. He will not permit himself to be used as a means to any end extraneous to his own essence, no matter how lofty the goal may be: God, Life, or Fatherland. Every poet, at the moment he starts his career, must choose between putting his personality at the service of Poetry, or using poetry to exalt his personality. An involuntary decision, but obligatory. From that time on, the die is cast."[3]

Yet at the time that Alfonsina published her first collection of poetry, there were still a good many writers who held to the pre-Modernist notion that literature should be a weapon in a social or political struggle. They criticized her poetry for not being "engagé," and Alfonsina was caught in the cross fire. She was once asked in an interview what she thought of those who accused her of writing poetry that they deemed "useless" because it was not combative and did not follow the banners of any credo—poetry, in short, whose flowers never ripened into fruit. "From the spiritual point of view," she retorted, "I see no reason why fruit should be more useful than flowers. A flower is useful because it is beautiful. And there have been times when the contemplation of a rose has been of greater benefit to me than a book of moral and philosophical maxims."[4]

Although her answer reflects a perfectly legitimate Modernist orientation, the great majority of the poems in her early work are basically traditional in style and personal in theme. She was acquainted with the French Symbolist poets, Charles Baudelaire and Paul Verlaine, and she was a great admirer of the Nicaraguan poet, Rubén Darío, but their influence on her poetry was only superficial. She went her own way and created her own aesthetic ideal, which she once described as "an attempt to mix art and life, and to learn to scorn death while still of sound mind, body, and spirit."[5]

Because Alfonsina published her first volumes of poetry at a time when Modernism was thought to be on the wane, she is generally considered to be a "Post-Modernist" by most critics. This seems to be a catchall term for the poet who cannot easily be categorized either as a Modernist or as a member of the avant-garde of the 1920s. Her last two collections of poetry, however, show the unquestionable influence of these postwar experimenters, for she consciously sought new modes of self-expression to break her former patterns. In direct contrast to her earlier works, these two volumes, *El mundo de siete pozos (The World of Seven Wells)* and *Mascarilla y trébol (Mask and Clover)*, published in 1934 and 1938 respectively, put new stress on form rather than content. Like other avant-garde poets, she made a radical departure from traditional styles and adopted, for the first time in her work, the free verse form. Gone is the emotional tone of her former poetry, which she replaced with impersonal, objective themes and abstract ideas. Some of the poems in her last volume were so obscure that she wrote explanatory footnotes to accompany them, but a friend persuaded her to omit them from the published collection.

Alfonsina was inevitably subject to the various literary influences of her time and place, and, like any good poet, she created a body of work that was personal and distinctive, but by no means easily definable according to the dicta of schools, movements, manifestos, credos, and the like. In her last recorded public lecture, given at the University of Montevideo in 1938, she was called upon to describe her own poetry and how she came to write it. She found the task to be almost impossible. After explaining that she wrote her first volume of poems simply as a way to avoid dying while she was working at a desk job, she then tackled the problem of describing her verses by asking questions rather than giving answers: "Was my poetry just a form of rebellion, a way to communicate my discomfort? Did it give expression to an inner voice which had long been muffled? Did it reflect my thirst for justice, my longing to be in love with love, or was it a little music box that I had in my hand and which played all by itself, whenever it wanted to, without ever being stabbed by a key? At any rate, is not the poet a phenomenon which offers few variations, a subtle antenna which receives voices from nobody knows where, and then translates them nobody knows how?"[6] Quite predictably she made no attempt to answer these questions. Instead, she allowed her poetry to speak for itself.

I   La inquietud del rosal (The Disquietude of the Rosebush)

La inquietud del rosal, Alfonsina's first collection of verse, was published in 1916. Most of the poems had been written in haste, on scraps of paper or on the back of telegram forms, during working hours, at home, or in cafés. They were composed at a time when she was living under great stress. She was an unmarried mother with a new baby, her work was boring, she was underpaid, she had just moved to Buenos Aires from the provinces, she had no friends, and she was separated from the man she loved. "Even so," she said in an interview, "I didn't lie down and die. I found new energy in the very depths of my body and soul, and I used it to cure my spiritual wounds. I threw myself right back into the struggle with great faith in the future, using as my banner my unshakable love. It was then that I composed my first poems. I wrote about all the suffering, longing, and dreams which were making my life miserable in spite of my efforts to overcome them. And so, with the same sort of disorientation that seemed to be at the root of my unhappiness, I published my first book, which today frankly embarrasses me. I would love to be able to destroy every single copy of that book until there was not a single trace of it left."[7]

The critics, however, were not always as harsh with her as she was with herself. In one of the earliest known commentaries on her poetry, Nicolás Coronado wrote that she was "capable of understanding and communicating lyric beauty. Even though she does not yet possess the mental flexibility and richness of verbal expression that a definitive work requires, there is no doubt that her book offers the promise of future productions that will be profound and long-lasting . . . .If she occasionally shocks the reader by dealing with some rather unseemly subjects, it should not be taken as a deliberate attempt on her part to call attention to herself. Miss Storni, we repeat, is a poet, and as such she openly displays her emotions and emphasizes the impressions she receives from her contemplation of things. There is no question that the book has many defects. Her verses are sometimes uneven and incorrect, and she says ingenuous and puerile things which lack poetic value. But there are still some really beautiful poems in this book . . . .She has not yet achieved her potential, but she will some day present the world with more than one valuable literary creation."[8]

Alfonsina wrote this book before she had a chance to assimilate the very real pain she felt during her first years in Buenos Aires. She had not yet been able to put her suffering into the proper perspective, she was too close to her own problems, and consequently her attempts to sublimate her experience were infelicitous. The results were poems that were often melodramatic and sentimental, reflecting not so much the influence of Romanticism, as has often been stated, as they did the simple misery of a young woman, barely past her adolescence, who was as yet unprepared to create anything of real artistic value. Nor had she done much serious reading at that point in her life. Although she had no doubt acquainted herself with the work of some Modernist poets, as mentioned above, she could not have gone so far as to incorporate influences from "all the poetic schools that have succeeded each other from the Romantics right on down to the decadent swans,"[9] a claim made by Roberto Giusti and repeated by many other critics through the years. In 1972 León Benarós published for the first time a letter written by Alfonsina to her friend Juan Julián Lastra shortly after *La inquietud del rosal* appeared, in which she states:

Many people have accused me of being influenced by poets I have never read. Even Lugones, talking to me about the book, told me that he had noticed a very obvious influence from the most fashionable French poets.

So as not to appear ignorant, I did not ask him who they were, but the truth is that I work nine hours a day locked up in an office, so in the period of time that it took me to write the poems that were collected in this volume, I never had a chance to read much of anything at all. My poems were all born of a moment of great anguish, and they are absolutely free of the influence of any models.[10]

That her early poems were totally free of literary influences of any kind is clearly an exaggerated claim, but it is no doubt true that her "moment of great anguish" gave rise to some mawkish verse which brings to mind the Romantic period at its worst. The promise was there, as Coronado was astute enough to point out, but most critics prefer simply to overlook this first volume altogether. Alfonsina was more than willing to do the same, for as she exclaimed in her last lecture in Montevideo: "God deliver you, my friends, from *La inquietud del rosal!*"[11]

II   El dulce daño (Sweet Pain)

Alfonsina's second collection of poetry, *El dulce daño,* was published in 1918. Her verse was still largely a reflection of her suffering, which she expressed in unreserved terms: "I made the book thus:/ Sighing, weeping, dreaming, alas for me!" ("Hice el libro así:/ Gimiendo, llorando, soñando, ay de mí!")[12] The main theme is introduced in "Este grave daño" ("This Grievous Pain") where she states that:

the grievous pain she feels is a sweet pain, for the memory of her departure, which ought to be far removed from her life, still remains within her. Roses grow from her hands, but so many butterflies are sipping their nectar that they, as well as the poet, will soon be dried out.

> Este grave daño, que me da la vida
> Es un dulce daño la partida
> Que debe alejarse de la misma vida
> Más cerca tendré.
>
> Yo llevo las manos brotadas de rosas,
> Pero están libando tantas mariposas
> Que cuando por secas se acaben mis rosas,
> Ay, me secaré.
>
> *El dulce daño,* p. 84

Her bittersweet disillusionment with love is balanced by several poems that express for the first time a young woman's earthy joy of life.

In "Sábado" ("Saturday") she tells of how she arose early one morning, ran barefoot through the house, and kissed the flowers in the garden. In a jubilant moment of self-renewal she lay down on the grass and drank in the clean vapors of the earth, then bathed herself in the fountain. She perfumed herself with the sweet-smelling water, while herons tickled her as they stole golden crumbs. Then, wearing a filmy gown, she listened to the sound of breakfast preparations as she contemplated the dazzling reflection of the sun on the marble stairs. Her eyes fixed themselves on the iron grill work, and once more the echo of sweet pain: she was waiting for *him*.

> Levanté temprano y anduve descalza
> Por los corredores; bajé a los jardines
> Y besé las plantas;
> Absorbí los vahos limpios de la tierra,
> Tirada en la grama;
> Me bañé en la fuente que verdes achiras
> Circundan. Más tarde, mojados de agua
> Peiné mis cabellos. Perfumé las manos
> Con zumo oloroso de diamelas. Garzas
> Quisquillosas, finas,
>
> De mi falda hurtaron doradas migajas,
> Luego puse traje de clarín más leve
> Que la misma gasa.
> De un salto ligero llevé hasta el vestíbulo
> Mi sillón de paja.
>
> Fijos en la verja mis ojos quedaron,
> Fijos en la verja.
> El reloj me dijo: diez de la mañana.
> Adentro un sonido de loza y cristales:
> Comedor en sombra; manos que aprestaban
> Manteles.
>   Afuera, sol como no he visto
> Sobre el mármol blanco de la escalinata.
> Fijos en la verja siguieron mis ojos,
> Fijos. Te esperaba.
>
> *El dulce daño*, pp. 84–85

In this poem Alfonsina accomplished what was to become a
hallmark of her later work: the creation of a poetic world based on
scenes taken from everyday reality. The refined aristocratic setting,
with its fountain and herons, brings to mind the imagery of the
Modernists, but the wicker chair and the breakfast dishes were
typical of the sort of objects that were to reappear often in her
poetry. Like some of her contemporaries, she refused to make a
distinction between "poetic" and "prosaic" vocabulary. She did not
separate her inner and outer world—if a chair inspired a poetic
association in her mind, then the chair appeared as part of the
resultant creation. She was not concerned about whether a chair was
more or less poetic than a swan.

Nor was she concerned, apparently, about whether or not it was
considered fitting for a young lady unblushingly to express her
amorous yearnings. Her poem "Sábado" already suggests, in a most
subtle and delicate way, what was to become a constantly recurring
theme in her poetry: the unfulfilled desire for love. Her critics,
however, found nothing subtle or delicate in the way she expressed
this theme, and they frowned on what they called her "erotic" verses. This provoked an indignant response from Alfonsina, who accused them of "intellectual and moral insufficiency" for not understanding that poetry is above such considerations. In retrospect the
whole matter seems like a tempest in a teapot, for a reading of *El
dulce daño* reveals nothing much more "erotic" than verses such as
"yo que al amarte te mordí" ("I who bit you when we made love").[13]
The "intellectual insufficiency" and narrow-minded opinions of
those in a position to judge her, however, help to explain how she
acquired a reputation for being a combative, embittered woman, for
their insensitive criticism never failed to make her furious.

Her attitude of defiance constitutes a theme that can be traced
throughout her first volumes.

It appears in *El dulce daño* in such poems as "Oveja descarriada" ("Lost
Sheep"), where the poet shrugs her shoulders when she is told she has gone
astray, and agrees with her accuser. She is proud to be a sheep who has
wandered away from a herd whose values she cannot respect.

> Oveja descarriada, dijeron por ahí.
> Oveja descarriada. Los hombros encogí.
>
> En verdad descarriada. Que a los bosques salí;
> Estrellas de los cielos en los bosques pací.

En verdad descarriada. Que el oro que cogí
No me duró en las manos y a cualquiera lo di.

En verdad descarriada, que tuve para mí
El oro de los cielos por cosa baladí.

En verdad descarriada, que estoy de paso aquí.

El dulce daño, p. 130

In this poem she uses the technical device of repetition not only to emphasize her ironic triumph at having gone astray, but also to accentuate the monotony of the life she rejected. She uses this stylistic technique even more successfully in another poem, "Cuadros y ángulos" ("Squares and Angles"), which is curiously reminiscent of the modern grievance against cheaply built houses that all look just the same.

Not only are the houses all alike, complains the poet, but the people in them have square souls, and their ideas are all lined up in rows. She is surprised to realize that she has been contaminated herself, for while contemplating this spectacle, she discovers that she has wept a square tear.

Casas enfiladas, casas enfiladas,
Casas enfiladas.
Cuadrados, cuadrados, cuadrados.
Casas enfiladas.
Las gentes ya tienen el alma cuadrada,
Ideas en fila
Y ángulo en la espalda.
Yo misma he vertido ayer una lágrima,
Dios mío, cuadrada.

El dulce daño, p. 131

In many ways this poem is the cornerstone of the whole structure of ideas that Alfonsina wanted to communicate. Most of the outrage she expressed in her writing stemmed from the fact that she was invariably misunderstood because so many people had stereotyped ideas about women, just as they had about everything else in their world of "squares and angles." All through her poetry, and throughout her prose as well, Alfonsina implored men to give up thinking of women as charming little playthings, for until this was accomplished, there could be no hope of elevating the relationship between the sexes to a point where there could be some real communication and mutual appreciation. But many of her critics, from

her day right down to the present time, tended to misinterpret the
anger, exasperation, and disillusionment they saw in her poetry,
assuming that it was nothing more than a manifestation of the impo-
tent rage of a frustrated female. César Fernández Moreno, a recognized poet himself and a friend of Alfonsina's, nevertheless showed a
surprising lack of understanding in his criticism of her poetry.
"Generally speaking, poetry written by women, like women themselves, is more conditioned by their sex than that written by
men . . .the overly shrill cynicism and true bitterness of many of
her poems demonstrate that Alfonsina never found the deep and
lasting love that should have been a correlation to the kind she
occasionally describes so openly. This lack of a profound relationship
caused her to place her feminine problems in the foreground of her
work, as a substitution [for what she was missing]."[14] He goes on to
say that she views women as inferior beings, subjected by the pa-
triarchy. In order to prove this extraordinary allegation, he selects a
poem from *El dulce daño* which he believes to be a perfect illustra-
tion of Alfonsina's opinion of women.

In reality, this poem is an extremely ironic description of the poet's
observation of how men themselves see women as silly butterflies flitting
around a garden, tasting every flower, flirting indiscriminately; women, in
short, with nothing in their heads but a little straw.

> Sí, vanas mariposas sobre jardín de enero,
> Nuestro interior es todo sin equilibrio y huero.
> Luz de cristalería, fruto de carnaval
> Decorado en escamas de serpientes del mal.
> Así somos,¿no es cierto? Ya lo dijo el poeta:
> Movilidad absurda de inconsciente coqueta.
> Deseamos y gustamos la miel de cada copa
> Y en el cerebro habemos un poquito de estopa.
>   From "Capricho," *El dulce daño*, p. 88

Alfonsina certainly did not see women, as a whole, as being inferior to men, nor did she believe that men in general were inferior
to women. What she deplored in men, however, was their tendency
to think they were the superior sex and to treat women in a super-
cilious or condescending way. Although she refused to make general
judgments based on sex alone, she sensed that as an individual she
was more intelligent than the majority of men she knew, so she felt

humiliated when they simply took it for granted that she was "just a woman." The difficulty was particularly burdensome when it came to mattters of love. "I am superior to most of the men around me," she once wrote to a friend, "but physically, as a woman, I am their slave, their mold, like clay in their hands. I cannot love them freely—I have too much pride to submit myself to them."[15]

III Irremediablemente (Irremediably)

Her comments in the above letter are almost a paraphrase of one of her best-known poems, "Hombre pequeñito" ("Little Man"), which appeared in her third volume of poetry, *Irremediablemente*, published in 1919.

Here she demands that the "little man" let her out of the cage in which he has kept her. Since he has treated her as though she were a canary, the time has come for her to fly away. She calls him "little" because he does not understand her, nor is there any likelihood that he ever will. She cannot understand him either, and she tells him not to expect any more than the half hour of love she has given him.

Hombre pequeñito, hombre pequeñito,
Suelta a tu canario que quiere volar . . .
Yo soy el canario, hombre pequeñito,
Déjame saltar.

Estuve en tu jaula, hombre pequeñito,
Hombre pequeñito que jaula me das.
Digo pequeñito porque no me entiendes,
Ni me entenderás.

Tampoco te entiendo, pero mientras tanto
Abreme la jaula que quiero escapar;
Hombre pequeñito, te amé media hora.
No me pidas más.

Irremediablemente . . ., pp. 165–166

"Hombre pequeñito" appears in the second half of the collection, along with other poems whose general themes are based on the poet's disillusionment with love. The first half of the volume is in direct contrast with the second in that it includes a good number of poems that express her very powerful and passionate feelings for her lover, in whom she places all her hopes and expectations. She is

deeply distressed, however, to discover that all her loves turn "irremediably" to ashes almost before she has an opportunity to enjoy
them. She is not yet experienced enough to know that this is in the
very nature of passionate love, so she tends either to blame the man
for failing her, as in "Hombre pequeñito," or to blame herself for
failing him, as in "¡Ayme!" ("Ah, me!"), where she laments the fact
that her soul has turned to stone just when she is offered the love of
a kind and sensitive man.

> Y te dejé marchar calladamente,
> A ti, que amar sabías y eras bueno,
> Y eras dulce, magnánimo y prudente.
>
> . . . Toda palabra en ruego te fue poca,
> Pero el dolor cerraba mis oídos . . .
> Ah, estaba el alma como dura roca.
>
> *Irremediablemente* . . . , p. 176

Passionate love is born in the mind and fed by the imagination. As
long as the beloved is unattainable, then, the lover can enjoy the
illusion of being in love. But once passion is transplanted to the
world of reality it inevitably dies sooner or later, and the lover is
bereft not so much of the beloved, as of the feeling of passion itself.
The irony is that these dreams of love are often remembered as the
most powerful and exciting experiences of a lifetime. They have
inspired some of the greatest creations of art and literature, and
most lyric poetry, like that of *El dulce daño* and *Irremediablemente*,
is an expression of the bittersweet character of passionate love and
the painful disillusionment it irremediably engenders.

Alfonsina communicated these experiences with an unblushing
frankness and an eloquent simplicity that were greatly admired by
some critics. Luis María Jordán, writing about *Irremediablemente*
shortly after it was published in 1919, stated in his opening lines that
the poetry of this strong woman, all dreams, flesh, and emotion, was
exceptional in a country overpopulated with "lyrical Jeremiahs and
effeminate rhymesters."[16] And further on: "How far she is from the
almost Byzantine versifiers common among us, who, because they
dare not express themselves or have nothing to say, give us in cold
and perfect stanzas the pale trickery of their emotionless rhetoric or
their worthless imitations!" In direct contrast to the opinions of a
poet like Jorge Luis Borges, who today deplores Alfonsina's use of

everyday vocabulary in her poetry,[17] Jordán praised her for calling things by their names: "Her language is not contaminated by words [taken directly from] French, English, Italian, or Latin. She writes in Castilian, in our sonorous and harmonious Peninsular tongue, without torturing it with false and borrowed adornments. To this we must attribute, no doubt, her diaphanous clarity."[18]

Alfonsina was slowly establishing herself as a bold and independent poet. The reviews that appeared in journals and newspapers were becoming more favorable, and many of the preconceived notions that her critics had held about women poets were beginning to be dispelled by her obvious talent. She was at last succeeding in changing the stereotyped opinions of those unenlightened minds who would have automatically relegated her work to the "women's pages" if she herself had not fought so stubbornly for the recognition she deserved. She saw her victory not in terms of a personal triumph, but as one that could benefit women as a whole. She expressed this idea in one of her best-known poems, "Bien pudiera ser . . ." ("It Could Well Be . . ."), which appeared in the final pages of *Irremediablemente*.

It could well be that everything I have expressed in verse is nothing more than what never came to be," says the poem, "nothing more than something that was hidden and repressed family after family, woman after woman. They say that where my people came from, everything that had to be done was carefully weighed out . . . . They say that the women on my side were all silent . . . Oh, it could well be . . . Occasionally my mother would feel like liberating herself, but then a profound sorrow would ascend into her eyes, and she would weep in the shadows. And everything that was corroded, defeated, mutilated, everything that was closed up inside her soul, I liberated it all myself, I think, without meaning to."

Pudiera ser que todo lo que en verso he sentido
No fuera más que aquello que nunca pudo ser,
No fuera más que algo vedado y reprimido
De familia en familia, de mujer en mujer.

Dicen que en los solares de mi gente, medido
Estaba todo aquello que se debía hacer . . .
Dicen que silenciosas las mujeres han sido
De mi casa materna . . . Ah, bien pudiera ser . . .

A veces en mi madre apuntaron antojos

De liberarse, pero, se le subió a los ojos
Una honda amargura, y en la sombra lloró.
Y todo eso mordiente, vencido, mutilado,
Todo eso que se hallaba en su alma encerrado,
Pienso que sin quererlo lo he libertado yo.

Irremediablemente . . . , p. 188

IV Languidez (Languor)

Just as *El dulce daño* expresses both the pleasure and the suffering of passionate love, and *Irremediablemente* focuses on the feeling
of disillusionment that inevitably follows, so *Languidez* is generally
speaking a description of the poet's attempts to renounce the passion that caused her so many disappointments. Published in 1920,
Languidez followed her second and third volumes in close succes-
sion. Together these three collections of poetry could well be considered a trilogy dedicated to the three fundamental stages of passionate love: hope, with its attendant pain and exaltation, then disillusionment, and finally, renunciation. In the light of this theory one
can better understand Alfonsina's otherwise enigmatic prologue to
Languidez: "This book ends a modality of mine. If life and circumstances permit, my future poetry will be entirely different." She
later proved this statement to be true, for after publishing four
volumes in five years, she closed the parenthesis of this stage of her
life and did not publish another book of poetry until five years later.
During those five years of silence she meditated and matured, and
leaving behind the strident, overemotional tone so typical of the
poems that appeared in the trilogy, she published *Ocre (Ocher)* in
1925, a book that is universally considered to be her best work.
"This collection initiates," she continued in the prologue to *Languidez*, "the abandonment of subjective poetry, which cannot be
continued when the soul has stated, in respect to itself, all that it
had to say, at least in one sense." She had lived the three stages of
passionate love, she had expressed every feeling and emotion associated with the various phases, and she could not go back to the
beginning again. This final book in the trilogy might well be considered the supreme expression of her loss of innocence.

In this context one might also better understand an unusual poem
from *Languidez* which has sometimes puzzled critics. It is an extensive composition in free verse called "Carta lírica a otra mujer"

("Lyrical Letter to Another Woman"), in which the poet addresses the woman who has fallen in love with the man whom she herself secretly desires. There is no expression of jealousy or bitterness, for she understands that the other woman did not knowingly rob her of her unspoken hope. Instead, the poet talks to her gently and admiringly of her beauty, and of her good fortune in being loved by this man. She tells her that he could have belonged to her if she had only stretched out her hand, but that her soul was so dried up that she had no strength even to lift her arms.

> Acaso mía aquella dicha vuestra
> Me fuera ahora . . .¡sí! acaso mía . . .
> Mas ved, estaba el alma tan gastada
> Que el brazo mío no alcanzó a extenderse.
>
> *Languidez*, pp. 214-215

The poet's "worn out soul" is the key to the new tone which is evident everywhere in *Languidez*. She no longer has the strength to give herself freely to a new love, nor does she have the innocence to believe in the promise of happiness it offers. But in spite of the worldly knowledge she has acquired, she does not have the courage to abandon all thoughts of love, for the memory of passion's exaltation is too fresh in her mind. She becomes almost like an earthbound spirit, wandering about in a world which offers her nothing, but which she cannot give up.

> . . . yo, la que anduve
> Vagando por afuera de la vida,
> —Como aquellos filósofos mendigos
> Que van a las ventanas señoriales
> A mirar sin envidia toda fiesta—
>
> *Languidez*, p. 215

The poet finds a new and perhaps safer pleasure in identifying with the lovers rather than participating in an act which can no longer offer her any illusions. Thus she asks the other woman to let her kiss her hands in the same way and in the same places that her lover has kissed them, so that she may enjoy the "dreadful pleasure" of following the ineffable, passionate trail of his caresses. Her sentiment lacks any trace of envy because she has lost her belief in the divinity of Eros, and therefore she cannot truly wish to take the place of the other woman in her lover's embrace. At the same time, however, she longs to feel passion once more, so

the other woman becomes the barrier she needs, the ardent, live barrier which shields her from the dangers of love.

Now at last, says the poet, "I feel my bitter weariness begin to stir," and likewise, "this silence in my soul which gives me refuge, this mortal pain in which I submerge myself, this immobility of feeling," all disappear suddenly when "nothing is possible" any longer.

> Y allí en vos misma, sí, pues sois barrera,
> Barrera ardiente, viva, que al tocarla
> Ya me remueve este cansancio amargo,
> Este silencio de alma en que me escudo,
> Este dolor mortal en que me abismo,
> Esta inmovilidad del sentimiento
> ¡Que sólo salta, bruscamente, cuando
> Nada es posible!
>
> *Languidez*, p. 216

Most critics simply avoided discussing what they felt was a rather perverse attitude on the part of the poet. They limited themselves, instead, to praising her gallant generosity toward the other woman, whom they saw as her rival. Roberto Giusti wrote: "One of the most beautiful compositions of *Languidez* is 'Carta lírica a otra mujer,' the unknown rival, whose immense happiness the poet admires and envies without any resentment. The day that Alfonsina wrote this strange poem, resigned and sad, she used the most caressing words to evoke, with a somewhat morbid satisfaction, the lost love that she coveted. . . . This critic [referring to himself], without being an Othello, confesses that he cannot understand. Maybe women have the answer [Las mujeres dirán]."[19]

The answer, perhaps, is more likely to be found in a closer analysis of Alfonsina's reactions to the various stages of passion (hope, disillusionment, renunciation) which gradually emerge as a unified pattern from her poetic trilogy.[20] In this final phase she is struggling to renounce the intoxicating addiction which has caused her so much pain and which she now sees as pure vanity. But passion has its joy, too, and it is not easy to give it up, as she points out with unaccustomed levity in "Ligadura humana" ("Human Ties"):

Idiotic dream, who lives in my soul and keeps it warm, you are nestled
there like a poor beggar in a doorway . . . . I try in vain to get rid of you
every moment, but with your stupid persistence you come right back just as
often as I throw you out, you pesky fly.

> Imbécil sueño, que en el alma vives
> Guardándole calor;
> Estás acurrucado como un pobre
> Mendigo en un portón
>
> . . . .
> En vano te desplazo a cada rato:
> Con tu necio tesón,
> Cuantas veces te arrojo cuantas vuelves,
> Pesado moscardón.
>
> *Languidez*, p. 235

She is not entirely ready for renunciation, and her predicament is
universal. One is reminded of St. Augustine who, torn between his
desire to turn to religion and his conflicting sexual desires, once
prayed "Give me chastity and continence, only not yet." Alfonsina
has lost her once-innocent belief in the promises held out to her by
passionate love, so she restrains herself from becoming directly involved with her so-called rival's lover, but at the same time she is
unable to forget the "sweet pain" of love which cannot be erased
from her memory. Thus it is easy to see that the other woman is not
her rival, as so many have assumed, but rather a friend toward
whom the poet feels a gentle, affectionate superiority, as one who
has suffered more, seen farther, and gone beyond.

Alfonsina, however, had a tendency dating all the way back to her
childhood to be an *enfant terrible*, so when it became fashionable to
"shock the bourgeois," she was right in her element. Unfortunately
her desire to shock sometimes had the effect of obfuscating the real
meaning of her words. In a sonnet entitled "Esclava" ("Slave"), very
similar in theme to her "Carta lírica," she was not content merely to
trace the lover's kisses on the other woman's hand. Instead, she
closed the sonnet with the words "cuando la besas tú, beso su boca"
("when you kiss her, I kiss her lips"). This caused Roberto Giusti to
wonder "what strange sentiment attracts her to the gentle and
beautiful rival who was able to win for herself the desired caresses.
There is only one step from there to the immortal ode of Sappho."[21]
Small wonder that critics should have seen something perverse or

more than a little Sapphic in this line. The sonnet itself emphasizes
her suffering at seeing the couple together, but it does not specify
the cause of her pain, which, it is assumed, stems mainly from envy.
When the sonnet is placed in the entire context of the trilogy,
however, it is clear that her suffering stems not from envy, but from
the conflict between her rational decision to renounce passionate
love and her emotional desire to surrender to the "idiotic dream."
Feeling drained and disillusioned, then, Alfonsina turned her
thoughts to other forms of love. Poems dealing with filial, fraternal,
and maternal love are especially powerful in this volume. In "Han
venido" ("They Have Come"), the poet speaks of her mother who
goes to visit her one day.

She smiled at me the way people do when they know the human heart
very well; she put her two hands on my shoulders, she looked at me in-
tensely . . . and my tears flowed out.

> Mi madre ha sonreído como suelen
> Aquellos que conocen bien las almas;
> Ha puesto sus dos manos en mis hombros,
> Me ha mirado fijo . . .
> Y han saltado mis lágrimas.
>
> *Languidez*, p. 217

The poet sometimes describes people who are older and wiser than
she is, who see in her rather dramatic personality a foreshadowing of
unhappiness.

There is a paternal tenderness in "En una primavera" ("One Springtime")
in the attitude of the old man who tries to warn her to go slowly, prudently,
and not to let herself be scorched by her own fire. But she is young and
cannot listen; instead she tells him enthusiastically about the song of the
birds and the cool water. He puts his two hands gently on her forehead,
which mirrors her inner torment, and leaning forward he whispers, "Poor
child."

> Pequeña, ve despacio, mucho juicio,
> No te quemen tus llamas.
>
> Estaba yo a sus pies humildemente,
> Humildemente y toda yo temblaba.

—¡Cómo cantan los pájaros, le dije,
Cómo es de fresca el agua!
Sobre mi frente, espejo de tormentas,
Se detuvieron sus dos manos mansas;
Se inclinó sobre mí con un susurro:
—Pobrecita muchacha . . .

Languidez, p. 211

Alfonsina's own love for children is clearly evident in a number of poems in this volume, particularly in one called "Miedo," ("Fright") where the poet cradles a frightened child in her arms. The little boy's subsequent relief is described with great simplicity: "Luego el niño levanta la cabeza, me mira/Con sus ojos azules y muy quedo suspira" ("Then the child raises his head, gazes at me with his blue eyes, and very quietly sighs"). It is through her contemplation of children that it slowly begins to dawn on her that the disillusionment she feels cannot apply generally to the whole human species. In her poem called "La belleza" ("Beauty"), she describes the fear she experiences when she suspects that somehere within the children who surround her there lies a bad seed. But suddenly the window blows open and the whole scene is bathed in the light of the blue sky, as though something were trying to prove the error of her thoughts.

Hands that I cannot see set free my soul anew; once more I can believe, and my grief is assuaged again. I say, without knowing why: Thank you!

Manos que yo no veo
El alma me desatan
De nuevo; nuevamente
Creo en algo: se aplaca
Mi amargura, y de nuevo,
Digo, sin entenderlo:
¡Gracias!

Languidez, p. 222

For the first time she seems to sense that this new freedom that she has glimpsed may provide her with a greater feeling of exaltation than that which she experienced when she was a slave to her passionate loves. She is now able, as never before, to go beyond the limited world of her self-oriented passions and extend her love to include all humanity. One of the poems that best expresses this new freedom is "El obrero" ("The Workman").

Here the poet describes herself as a typical product of her spiritually impoverished century, all dressed up in stylish clothes and expensive furs. She was strolling along a city street one day when suddenly a workman threw at her, like stones, a barrage of offensive comments. "I turned to him and put my hand on his shoulder. With a kind expression and gentle voice, I asked him slowly: 'Why did you say such things to me? I am your sister.' " The workman was strong, but she could see that his heart was timid and kind, and that her attitude had won him over. The people who passed by stared at the well-dressed woman and the workman as they stood hand in hand, bound together by their mutual forgiveness and an infinite human understanding.

> Mujer al fin y de mi pobre siglo,
> Bien arropada bajo pieles caras
> Iba por la ciudad, cuando un obrero
> Me arrojó, como piedras, sus palabras.
>
> Me volví a él; sobre su hombro puse
> La mano mía: dulce la mirada,
> Y la voz dulce, dije lentamente:
> —¿Por qué esa frase a mí? Yo soy tu hermana.
>
> Era fuerte el obrero, y por su boca
> Que se hubo puesto sin quererlo, blanda,
> Como una flor que vence las espinas
> Asomó, dulce y tímida, su alma.
>
> La gente que pasaba por las calles
> Nos vio a los dos las manos enlazadas
> En un solo perdón, en una sola
> Como infinita comprensión humana.
>
> *Languidez*, p. 223

Probably the workman's smile had less to do with infinite human understanding than it did with the fact that holding hands with the well-dressed lady was the best thing that had happened to him all day. In spite of its naïveté, however, this poem should be seen as an expression of the poet's new desire to seek freedom from the self, an assertion which she clearly states in the prologue of *Languidez*.

V   Ocre (Ocher)

Five years were to pass between the publication of *Languidez* and the appearance of Alfonsina's fifth collection of poetry, which came out in 1925. She called the book *Ocre*, but, as Baldomero Sanín Cano reports, she could just as easily have called it *Purple*, or *Pink*, or *Green*.[22] She believed that books of poetry, like musical compositions, should be identified simply by numbers or letters. "If the present volume had been given a code number, however," wrote Sanín, "to differentiate it from its predecessors and possible successors, the public would probably have invented *Ocre* as a reference title, because a large part of the book is spiritually bathed in tones of that color. As for me, I would have chosen the title *Irridescence*, in order to try to capture its cerebral atmosphere."[23]

If, in general terms, it can be said that *Languidez* focuses on that moment of insight which led the poet to attempt a conscious renunciation of passion, then *Ocre* is in many ways a testimony to her failure. Instead, she resigns herself to the age-old struggle to harmonize the conflicting demands of reason and instinct, and from her personal defeat there emerges an artistic victory. Just as the underlying tone of the trilogy was emotional, so the fundamental atmosphere in *Ocre* is cerebral, as Sanín rightly asserted. In the early collections the poet was the protagonist of the various dramas that unfolded. But in this volume something entirely new has happened: she has stepped outside herself, so to speak, and has become the rather analytical observer of her own life. She now views herself from a distance, with a perspective that allows her to place herself within a larger framework. In the opening poem of *Ocre*, "Humildad" ("Humility"), which sets the tone for most of the volume, she describes the persona as a frail human being.

There was a time, she explains, when she proudly dealt in the false currency of her verses, thinking them to be examples of a glorious intellectual harvest. "But be patient, obscure woman," she tells herself ironically, for she knows that the time will come when the great Destructive Force, which devours everything, will completely wipe out her presence. He will descend among her yellowed books, and lifting her up with his fingers, he will puff up his cheeks just slightly, and with an air of infinite boredom he will blow her away, like so much chaff, into the realm of oblivion.

> Yo he sido aquélla que paseó orgullosa
> El oro falso de unas cuantas rimas

Sobre su espalda, y creyó gloriosa,
De cosechas opimas.

Ten paciencia, mujer que eres oscura:
Algún día, la Forma Destructiva
Que todo lo devora,
Borrará mi figura.

Se bajará a mis libros, ya amarillos,
Y alzándola en sus dedos, los carrillos
Ligeramente inflados, con un modo

De gran señor a quien lo aburre todo,
De un cansado soplido
Me aventará al olvido.

Ocre, p. 259

This new image of herself as an insignificant creature at the mercy
of forces she cannot control reappears several times in *Ocre*. In the
sonnet entitled "Inútil soy" ("I Am Useless"), she describes how she
had once wanted to accomplish something worthwhile,

"but, bound to the seductive fantasies of my instinct, I returned to the dark
well. For, like some lazy, voracious insect, I was born to love."

Pero, atada al ensueño seductor
De mi instinto volví al oscuro pozo,
Pues, como algún insecto perezoso
Y voraz, yo nací para el amor.

Ocre, p. 276

Every capitulation to love is seen as a failure: "Traiciono a cada
instante sin querer" ("I betray each instant against my will"),[24]
which happens in spite of herself: "Ay, quiero estarme quieta y soy
movida" ("Oh, I would like to remain still, and yet I am moved").[25]
She greets each new love with jaded familiarity: "Es una boca más la
que he besado./ ¿Qué hallé en el fondo de tan dulce boca?/ Que
nada hay nuevo bajo el sol . . ." ("I have kissed yet another mouth.
What did I discover in the depths of such a sweet mouth? That there
is nothing new under the sun . . .").[26]

There still exists the old cynicism and the disillusionment with man's
egotism, as when she complains of having descended to the very depths of
her lover's soul, only to shiver in the icy wind of his frozen ego.

¿De qué me quejo? Es cierto que me bajé hasta el fondo
Del alma del que amaba, y lleno de sí mismo
Lo hallé, y al viento helado de su helado egoísmo
Dudé que el globo fuera, como dicen, redondo.

Ocre, p. 280

And yet the cynical disillusionment expressed in *Ocre* has lost the bitterness it had in the trilogy. The poet has grown older, and she no longer blames her lover for falling short of her ideal: "No eres tú el que me engañas; quien me engaña es mi sueño" ("It is not you who are deceiving me; I am being deceived by my own dream").[27] Her experience and insight into the ways of men have given her a sense of humor that was almost entirely absent from previous collections of poetry, as in the "Divertidas estancias a don Juan" ("Amusing Stanzas to Don Juan"):

She advises the legendary lover not to visit the modern world because he would have no success at all with the sophisticated, well-read women of Buenos Aires, many of whom have acquired the necessary skills to beat him at his own game.

Las muchachas leídas
De este siglo de hervor
Se mueren aburridas
Sin un cosechador.
Más que nunca preciosas,
Oh gran goloso, están.
Mas no ceden sus rosas.
No despiertes, don Juan.
. . . .
Y hasta hay alguna artera,
Juguetona mujer,
Que toma tu manera
Y ensaya tu poder.

Ocre, p. 292

The hopes and fantasies that were once the foundation of her poetic world have now evaporated, but her memory of them remains in the foreground. The formerly bitter sarcasm with which she expressed her disappointment has now changed to the light-hearted irony of a woman who has decided, finally, to accept reality for whatever it may be. Her feminine nature obliges her to surrender herself to the male of the species, for better or for worse, so she accepts her role with sarcastic resignation. In "Saludo al hombre" ("Salute to Man"), she bows down in mock reverence to man, whose usurpation of the throne of humankind has never posed any serious problem to him. He takes it for granted that he is the superior sex, and that his divine rights are beyond dispute. "If that is your game," the poet seems to say, "then so be it." Then, raising her glass: "Brindo por tu adiestrada libertad, la soltura/ Con que te sientes hijo claro de la natura" ("I toast your ability to be free, the ease with which you see yourself as Nature's favorite son").

Not all critics saw in *Ocre* a reflection of a new maturity on the part of the poet which allowed her to view herself and those around her in less dramatic, more realistic terms. Carmen Sidonie Rosenbaum, in her largely excellent chapter on Alfonsina, sees her as even more embittered than before: "In this book she is more bitter, yet more resigned to the poverty of her spiritual and amorous life. Her taunts at men are more caustic; her attitude more ironic. Her spirit, with the vintage of experience, has assumed the ocher or faded tone of aridity rather than the honeyed and mellow one of fruitfulness. Her laughter is more raucous and rings less true. She takes whatever love—whatever life—is meted out to her, with spiritual and moral listlessness, for she is weary of hoping and of waiting. . . . She knows man to be faithless, vain, selfish, yet she continues to be cognizant of the power he has over her—for she cannot free herself from the need of the 'rey devorante' ('devouring king'). But, rather than with resignation, she meets failure with cynicism, with irony, or with feigned indifference."[28]

While it is certainly true that her poetry is more cynical and ironic in *Ocre* than in the preceding volumes, a closer analysis suggests that she had long since abandoned her former resentment and bitterness when she acquired the maturity to see through the sham of human pretensions, including her own, and accept what life had to offer, even though it inevitably fell far short of her expectations. She learned to face reality, then, not with "moral and spiritual listlessness," but with the melancholy smile with which so many poets and writers have greeted their coming of age. Her taunts at man were indeed caustic, but she no longer blamed him for being what he was. Instead she smiled at his poses, while at the same time she felt saddened by the seemingly limitless ability of the earthbound human species to ignore the world of the mind and spirit.

VI   Poemas de amor (Love Poems)

Just when it seemed that Alfonsina had reached a philosophical pinnacle from which she could look down complacently at the spectacle of the human comedy, fate decided that she should fall in love again. There was nothing particularly extraordinary about the surrender of an emotional, imaginative woman to a passionate involvement, nor was there anything very unusual about the sentiments she expressed in the prose poems of which her new volume was comprised. The remarkable thing about *Poemas de amor*, published in 1926, is that it stands in such striking contrast to *Ocre*, which appeared only the year before. Perhaps no poem in *Ocre* can serve as a better example of this ironic contrast than "Fiesta," where the poet describes a group of nubile young creatures dancing near the beach under the stars. They believe the sweet nothings that their companions murmur to them, and in their happiness they imagine that life is beautiful. "Yo me vuelvo de espaldas," says the final tercet. "Desde un quiosco/ Contemplo el mar lejano, negro y fosco,/ Irónica la boca. Ruge el viento" ("I turn my back. From a kiosk I contemplate the distant, dark, and angry sea. My mouth is ironic. The wind roars").

In *Love Poems* Alfonsina drops her role as the cynical, solitary observer of other peoples' foolish illusions, and abruptly becomes an active participant in the sentimental dramas that had figured so prominently in her early books of verse. She no longer turns her back on the young women dancing under the stars. Instead, she feels a tender solidarity with them, for they share with her the ecstasy of passion. "Oh mujeres," she exclaims, "¿cómo no me habéis tomado las manos y dicho:—Ese que va allí es él. Vosotras que sois mis hermanas porque alguna vez el mismo aire os confundió el aliento, ¿cómo no me dijisteis nada de que existía?" ("Oh, women, how could you have passed him by without discovering him? How is it that you did not take my hands and say 'That man over there: It is he.'? You who are my sisters because you have been moved by the same spirit, how is it that you never told me he existed?").29

The book contains sixty-seven short compositions inspired, no doubt, by the style of Baudelaire's "petits poèmes en prose" ("little poems in prose"). The comparison can go no farther, however. The quality of Alfonsina's work in this volume is very uneven, ranging from mini-letters that are frankly sophomoric to paragraphs that do succeed in capturing a poetic moment. Perhaps part of the failure of these compositions can be attributed to the fact that they were written in a prose that turned out to be too prosaic for the content. Baudelaire set out to prove that poetry did not necessarily have to be written in verse, and while Alfonsina may have wished to emulate him,[30] her compositions give the impression of being poor prose translations of her poetry. Although some of her prose poems are more successful than others, as Janice Geasler Titiev has pointed out in her excellent stylistic analysis of this book,[31] there is nevertheless a general tendency to be overly direct and wordy. It is almost as if one were to replace the poetic and economical "To be or not to be" with a question like "Should I end it now, or should I go on living?"

Practically any one of her compositions can be chosen at random to illustrate this point. In poem XIX, for example, she says "Amo y siento deseos de hacer algo extraordinario. No sé lo que es. Pero es un deseo incontenible de hacer algo extraordinario. ¿Para qué amo, me pregunto, si no es para hacer algo grande, nuevo, desconocido?" ("I am in love and I feel like doing something extraordinary. I do not know what it is, but it is an uncontrollable desire to do something extraordinary. What is the use of loving, I ask myself, if not to do something great, new, unknown?")This sentiment rings true, of course, and has been expressed throughout literature. But despite the universality of the lover's urge to do great things, Alfonsina has reduced it here to a commonplace through her chatty, informal, and distinctly unpoetic style. One is left with the feeling that somehow her experiment has failed and that she could have put her talent to better use if she had written a sonnet on the same theme.

Alfonsina herself was not of that opinion, however. When asked in an interview which one of her books she liked best, she answered: "Of all my books, I have a preference for a small prose collection called *Love Poems*. I would not change one comma of it, even if I could improve it that way."[32] This statement was made in 1931, when she had had five years to put her prose poems into some sort of perspective, and still she felt that they represented her best literary effort. Her critics were strangely silent about the matter, preferring simply to ignore the book rather than attack it or defend it, but her readers enthusiastically endorsed her view, for they eventually bought up three editions. One is tempted to believe that there was something a bit suspect about its popularity, as if it might have appealed to people because they saw it as making a nice gift for a friend, or as being fine bedtime reading. However that may be, many readers were undoubtedly attracted by the same haughty spirit they had come to admire in her earlier works, as is attested by one of the best-known poems in prose which has been quoted extensively: "Tú, el que pasas, tú dijiste: ésa no sabe amar. Eras tú el que no sabías despertar mi amor. Amo mejor que los que mejor amaron." ("You, who are passing by, you said: she does not know how to love. But it was you who did not know how to awaken my love. I love better than all those who loved the best.")[33]

VII   Mundo de siete pozos (World of Seven Wells)

Nine more years were to go by after the appearance of *Ocre* before Alfonsina published her sixth volume of verse, *Mundo de siete pozos*, which came out in 1934. After completing *Ocre* she stated that she had no intention of writing verse any more, an announcement which disappointed and puzzled a good number of her critics. "Alfonsina Storni's reasons for sustaining such a proposal are of an intellectual nature," wrote Salomon Wapnir by way of explanation. "She observes that her verse, her present production, is rich in arguments and ideas resulting from her personal development, a circumstance which is leading her to seek more appropriate forms in which to express herself; the theater, for example."[34]

In the intervening years she indeed wrote several plays which expressed her attitudes toward society, tradition, and the role of the sexes, but by 1934 her interest in these topics had diminished considerably. Instead, she made a conscious effort to play down any theme that had directly to do with sentiment or emotion, and turned her attention to the so-called objective world outside the realm of her personal feelings. She was no longer interested in writing verse that would move the hearts of her readers; her major concern now was to startle their minds with unusual themes and images. This change, of course, did not take place overnight. Ever since *Languidez* there was a tendency to see life from a more objective viewpoint, but it was not until the publication of *Mundo de siete pozos* that this trend began to take precedence over what was once a highly subjective vision in the early works.

The title of the collection is a metaphor in which the world is seen as a human head, whose "seven wells" are the eyes, ears, nose, and mouth. This image sets the tone of the volume, which describes

man as being part of a larger universe, rather than being at the core
of the universe as he was in previous books of verse. Often the
various elements of nature occupy the foreground, while man takes
a secondary position in the poetic scheme of things. This new
perspective is expressed in "Y la cabeza comenzó a arder" ("And the
Head Began to Burn"), a poem, like most of the others in this book,
written in free verse. Here the personified moon talks to the poet
through the window: "De aquí no me muevo;/ te miro./ No quiero
crecer/ ni adelgazarme./ Soy la flor/ infinita/ que se abre/ en el
agujero/ de tu casa./ No quiero ya/ rodar/ detrás de/ las tierras/ que
no conoces,/ mariposa,/ libadora/ de sombras"—*Mundo de siete
pozos*, p. 311. ("I am not moving from here; I am watching you. I do
not want to wax or wane. I am the infinite flower which opens in the
hole of your house. I no longer want to roll behind the lands you do
not know, butterfly who sips the shadows.") The rest of the poem
describes a scene of pure fantasy, where the light of the moon makes
the head resting in the poet's hands burn like the stars in twilight,
whose reflection then lights up her hands, which, in turn, shed their
radiance on the houses of men and the forests of beasts. Janice
Geasler Titiev concludes, after a careful stylistic analysis of the
poem and a comparison of its images with similar ones in other
poems, that the reader should not be tempted to base any interpretation on the free associations that might suggest themselves. She
shares the position of the New Critics when she points out that the
poem "means what it says," and that "a principal part of the value
lies in the fantasy."[35]

The very fact that it has become necessary to warn the reader that
it is risky to hazard an interpretation of some of the poems in *Mundo
de siete pozos* is in itself indicative of the new character of the poet's
creation. Many of the poems have ceased to be a direct expression of
her feelings and opinions; they have become instead the reflection
of moods and dreams described with abstract symbols and occasionally obscure images. And yet Alfonsina's presence is still strongly
felt in this volume. Even in a poem like "Y la cabeza comenzó a
arder," one can recognize her spirit in the rebellious moon who
refuses to do what is expected of it, and who roguishly turns the
tables on the persona by speaking to her and watching her, instead
of being addressed and contemplated itself.

Once again the poet's attempt to be untrue to herself has ended in a predictable failure. We have seen how her conscious desire to disassociate herself from her instinctual drive also ended in failure, but the resulting tension gave rise to a new poetic expression in *Ocre*. Similarly, the most innovative poems in *Mundo de siete pozos* are those in which she tries to describe an "objective" world devoid of her own presence. Her failure to do so, however, allows the reader to perceive her in a new way, as though her accustomed image had been refracted by the poetic world she herself has created around her. In "Ojo" ("Eye") for example, she describes the first stars which timidly weep their unsavory light on the fixed pupil of the eye: "Tímidas/ las primeras estrellas/ lloran/ su luz insabora/ en la pupila fija." —*Mundo de siete pozos*, p. 310. What was once an expression of specific discontent in earlier collections is here described in the infinite sadness of the anonymous eye which looks out on the world. The city itself begins to reflect her own despair in "Calle" ("Street") where she speaks of a dismal alley flanked by high gray walls, whose doors and vestibules are like open mouths leading to human catacombs within: "Un callejón abierto/ entre altos paredones grises./ A cada momento/ la boca oscura de las puertas,/ los tubos de los zaguanes,/ trampas conductoras/ a las catacumbas humanas." —*Mundo de siete pozos*, p. 362.

One of the most shocking images of her despair, however, occurs in "El hombre" ("The Man"), the first of the series of sonnets with which she closes the volume. Here the reader recognizes the not unfamiliar expression of maternal love that appeared occasionally in other books of verse, as the poet describes a newborn baby's innocent awakening to the world around him. When he becomes a young man "he entwines instinct, dreams, and soul in whips of fire, he tosses them behind him, to the winds. And he sings. He lifts his gaze kilometers above him and sees the star. He is moved, exalted, he longs for it. A 'Hand' chops off the hand which he has raised":

Da una larga corrida sobre la tierra luego.
Instinto, sueño y alma trenza en lazos de fuego,
los suelta a sus espaldas, a los vientos. Y canta.

Kilómetros en alto la mirada le crece
y ve el astro, se turba, se exalta, lo apetece:
una Mano le corta la mano que levanta.
Mundo de siete pozos, p. 373

In tracing the trajectory of this theme of despair, one notices a stylistic change that takes place as the volume progresses. In "Ojo," one of the first poems in the book, the verses vary greatly in length, some having as many as nine syllables while others have as few as two. The short verses tend to focus attention on their content, with the result that the poem becomes a sort of catalogue of individual moments, each of which acquires a certain importance because it stands alone. One is forced, therefore, to acknowledge each part of the poem as a unit, and this serves to distract the attention from the whole. The reader is invited to give up the temptation to reason; instead, he must feel, hear, and see the images which dance in kaleidoscopic patterns. In "Calle," however, although the verses continue to be irregular (varying from three to eleven syllables), the majority of them are longer than those in "Ojo." What is more, the poet has largely eliminated the constant punctuation that added to the staccato quality of "Ojo," so the verses of "Calle" flow more smoothly and allow the reader to enter the poetic world without undergoing the constant interruption of duo-syllabic verses. It would seem as though Alfonsina were slowly allowing herself to be lured away from the totally flexible free verse form to a more rigorous stylistic pattern. Finally, toward the end of the collection, she makes use of her favorite structure, the sonnet, and the lyrical world which this form traditionally expressed emerges once again in her poetry.

This is not to say that lyricism was absent from the poems in free verse. One of the best-known poems in *Mundo de siete pozos* is a lively composition called "Danza irregular" ("Irregular Dance"). "En la punta de un látigo/ mi corazón/ danza una danza/ en tirabuzón." —*Mundo de siete pozos*, p. 346. ("On the tip of a whip my heart dances a corkscrew dance.") After these opening lines the poet describes how her heart bounces like a ball on the lawn, twirls like the golden tip of a Chinese magician's wand, jumps about like a naked, frozen flower on a fountain's water spout, and goes around the entire world like a spinning top. Finally she begs to be intercepted, for her heart is running away with her: "¡atajadme!/ que me alza/ mi corazón." Julieta Gómez Paz did an excellent study of the theme of dancing in Alfonsina's poetry, in which she exclaimed: "How Alfonsina swirls, runs, and jumps in her verses! One can just see her become weightless and rise right up off the ground. She knew the kind of intoxication produced by good health, spring, love.

In her moments of greatest exaltation she begged for help because her giddiness lifted her straight off the earth itself."[36]

In spite of everything that has been said about the general tone of each of her various collections, Alfonsina periodically bursts out of the pervasive mood of a book of verse and creates a poem in direct contrast to the others. Thus the tone of hope and illusion that defines so many of the poems in _El dulce daño_ is abruptly shattered from time to time by the insertion of a deeply cynical composition, or the desire for renunciation so prevalent in _Languidez_ is suddenly belied by the appearance of a sonnet glorifying love. In _Mundo de siete pozos_, (_World of Seven Wells_) whose title gave special emphasis to the human head, there are nevertheless a number of poems in which the poet's irrepressible heart springs up to challenge the cool world of the mind. In this volume of many contrasts, it is the poet's head that inspires verses such as those in "Pasión":

Some kiss the temples, some kiss the hands, others kiss the eyes, others kiss the mouth. But there is little difference between one and the other. They are not gods, what can you expect? They are just barely human.

> Unos besan las sienes, otros besan las manos,
> otros besan los ojos, otros besan la boca.
> Pero de aquél a éste la diferencia es poca.
> No son dioses, ¿qué quieres?, son apenas humanos.
>
> _Mundo de siete pozos_, p. 374

But the heart takes precedence over the mind in a poem like "Regreso en sueños" ("Return in Dreams") where the poet has a dream about a long-forgotten love:

Bird of the air, his mouth reposed on my night-darkened mouth. But it was not a mouth. It was like moss, macerated in God's suns.

> Pájaro de aire, reposó la boca
> sobre la boca mía anochecida.
> Mas no era boca. A musgo, macerado
> en los soles de Dios, se parecía.
>
> _Mundo de siete pozos_, p. 345

VIII   Marcarilla y trébol (Mask and Clover)

Four years after the appearance of _Mundo de siete pozos_, Alfonsina published her seventh and final book of verse, _Mascarilla y_ *trébol.* The year was 1938, the poet was forty-six years old, and her many readers and admirers were to be shocked and saddened by her suicide in late October of the same year. This new collection of verse was a testimony to the many changes that had taken place within her, and to the very different vision of the world which she had created as a result of her suffering. She foresaw that the book would be criticized by those who were accustomed to her old mode, for she knew they would no doubt be disappointed by her radical departure from the general atmosphere of her previous volumes of verse. In the "Breve Explicación ("Brief Explanation") which serves as a prologue to *Mascarilla y trébol*, she wrote: "Judging by the general opinion—not that of the minority—expressed concerning some poems from this book that were published in journals and newspapers, I foresee that it is going to be called obscure. . . . Naturally certain parts of this volume will require the imaginative, and to a certain degree creative collaboration of the reader. But is that not just what the . . . public is asking to do, to collaborate with the writer, the sculptor, the musician, etc.? The avant-garde movements both in art and politics are supported by this social collaboration, which is being demanded more and more all the time."

Roberto Giusti, in his well-known article published in *Nosotros* a month after her death, selected two of her worst poems as examples of her "obscurity." In one of them, entitled "Un diente" ("A Tooth"), he quotes her description of a tooth which "dio guerra/ a Rusia, Holanda, y a Noruega juntas" ("waged war on Russia, Holland, and Norway together").[37] He would not have found the answer to this riddle, he says, were it not for the fact that Alfonsina gave it to him herself in some explanatory notes which she had initially intended to include in the volume. In her notes she explained that the tooth was waging war on these countries because it was chewing caviar from Russia, cheese from Holland, and codfish from Norway. This information very quickly became a literary anecdote in critical circles, and soon *Mascarilla y trébol* became known as a collection of impossibly hermetic poems, just as their author had predicted.

A careful reading of this book, however, reveals a poetry that, far from "lacking soul" (Giusti's words),[38] expresses the poet's deeply felt insights into the meaning of her life. "In the last couple of years," said Alfonsina in the prologue, "some fundamental psychological changes have taken place within me. This is the key to the relatively new direction my poetry has taken, and not external literary currents which distort my true personality." It is fashionable to insist, nowadays, that the author's intentions and circumstances are irrelevant to the work of art, which must be allowed to speak for itself. Yet there is no question that this final book of verse can best be understood in the light of the poet's need to reexamine her personal values. The most original aspect of this volume is found in her quiet triumph over the heretofore incessant demands of her active and frustrating life, a life to which, for better or for worse, she had always dedicated herself entirely. And there is irony in her triumph: all her disillusionment, her cynicism, her insight, her resolutions to control the passion which she had so often seen as a cruel deception, all her mental efforts to negate her physical and sentimental needs met with failure, until she accepted her impending death and so saw life in an entirely new perspective. There is no inner conflict, no tension, no sign of struggle in *Mascarilla y trébol* as there was in every one of the preceding volumes—only a sorrowful understanding of the "vanity of vanities," an understanding devoid of her former anger and rebelliousness.

It was perhaps only natural that her totally new orientation should be expressed in a different style. Finding the traditional verse forms of her previous collections too restrictive, and feeling dissatisfied with the unlimited scope afforded by free verse, she invented a new verse form which she called the "anti-sonnet," but which Giusti more aptly called the "quasi-sonnet," since it was the same as the classical sonnet with its fourteen hendecasyllabic verses, except without rhyme.[39] The discipline of the traditional structure and the freedom of the unrhymed verse proved to be a happy combination. The sober, unconstrained hybrid offered her just the right medium in which to express her new perspective, which included both a minutely detailed description of a newly discovered microcosm and a panoramic view of the "outside" world and its symbolism. This intermixture of both a microscopic and telescopic vision of the so-called objective world is entirely new in Alfonsina's poetry, and many of her readers were disappointed to discover that her "subjective," passionate poems had vanished. "Her verse has gone from clear and musical to harsh and obscure," complained one of her critics,[40] and his opinion was echoed by another: "Yesterday's musicality has changed into a severe, harsh, and obscure poetry [which lacks] the grace and voluptuousness that used to be characteristic [of her previous volumes]."[41]

While these accusations have certainly proved to be largely un-justified, it is true that *Mascarilla y trébol* could be defined as anything but voluptuous. The first poem of the volume, "A Eros" ("To Eros"), is paradoxically the last time Alfonsina was to mention her lifelong struggle to dominate the puckish god, and his very absence from her subsequent poems attests to her victory.

Here she seizes Eros by the nape of the neck just as he is getting ready to shoot her with one of his arrows, and she shakes out his clockwork mechanism onto the beach. She carefully scrutinizes the little cogs and wheels and discovers the trap called sex. She contemplates him all spread out on the beach, surrounded by a group of startled sirens, while his god-mother of deceit, Lady Moon, climbs her albine slope. Then she hurls him into the mouth of the waves.

> He aquí que te cacé por el pescuezo
> a la orilla del mar, mientras movías
> las flechas de tu aljaba para herirme
> y vi en el suelo tu floreal corona.
>
> Como a un muñeco destripé tu vientre
> y examiné sus ruedas engañosas
> y muy envuelta en sus poleas de oro
> hallé una trampa que decía: sexo.
>
> Sobre la playa, ya un guiñapo triste,
> te mostré al sol, buscón de tus hazañas,
> ante un corro asustado de sirenas.
>
> Iba subiendo por la cuesta albina
> tu madrina de engaños, Doña Luna,
> y te arrojé a la boca de las olas.
>
> *Mascarilla y trébol*, p. 385

It is particularly interesting to compare this anti-sonnet with the one that appears at the very end of the book, entitled "A Madona Poesía" ("To Madonna Poetry"). The contrast is revealing: whereas Eros has been reduced to nothing more than a child's broken doll, Poetry has been placed on a pedestal and the poet offers her an atheist's prayer. She sees herself as a submissive sinner and she throws herself at the feet of Poetry, whose pure gaze she dares not meet with her own eyes and whose miraculous hand she feels un-worthy to touch.

"I place a small green branch on thy hem, with the humble intention of sinning less, by thy grace. It was no longer possible for me to live cut off from thy shadow, blinded as I was at birth by thy harsh irons."

> Una pequeña rama verdecida
> en tu orla pongo con humilde intento
> de pecar menos, por tu fina gracia,
>
> ya que vivir cortada de tu sombra
> posible no me fue, que me cegaste
> cuando nacida con tus hierros bravos.

Mascarilla y trébol, p. 418

The reader is left with the impression that Alfonsina was just about to start a new stage of her human journey, a stage which in many ways would have been ironically destined to approximate the one she had just completed. She started out by worshipping the god of love only to discover, finally, that passion was based on illusions and on repetitious situations which always led to the same dead end. When she realized that she had been mocked by the god who was actually no more than a mechanical toy, she struggled to rid herself of his unwelcome and yet attractive hold. But it was not until the last year of her life that she found a replacement for her idol, and she knelt before Poetry just as she had once bowed down to Passion. She had seen that passion as an end in itself was a trap. Had she lived, she might well have discovered that intellect as an end in itself was also a deception. If she had been able to complete the spiritual journey she had so courageously undertaken, she might have ended by losing herself instead of anxiously seeking self-fulfillment. But her presence is still very much in evidence in the last poem of her last collection, as she kneels in worship before what would have inevitably revealed itself, sooner or later, as one more illusion.

CHAPTER 3

The Playwright

I El amo del mundo (The Master of the World)

ALFONSINA'S first three-act play, *El amo del mundo*, opened in the Cervantes Theater in Buenos Aires on March 10, 1927. It closed three days later. The reasons for its failure were multiple, but most critics were unanimous in calling attention to the technical defects of the play, which were largely those of the typical beginner. Alfonsina quite obviously sat down and wrote the whole thing as the ideas occurred to her, without blocking out the scenes and action beforehand. As a result, she finished most of what she had to say by the beginning of the third act, so she found herself in the awkward position of having to cast around for material to use as padding. The audience, of course, became bored with the third act, which was undeniably anticlimactic. The other technical defect that was widely criticized had to do with the play's slow tempo and lack of action. The author had a message that she was anxious to convey, so she simply made her characters talk to one another about the various problems she had in mind, instead of creating a conflict that would allow the action to speak for itself. The spectators became tired of watching what was essentially two debating teams challenging each other. The play consequently failed as a play, but there is certainly no reason why it should not be remembered as a piece of extremely interesting literature. If its technical defects have caused it to be considered a mediocre play, then it might be more profitably considered a novel in dialogue form, for example. It would have been unfortunate indeed if *La Celestina*, which was also a novel in dialogue form, had been forgotten because it was thought to be insufficiently theatrical. The important thing is what Alfonsina said in this composition, and not the fact that she had not yet learned to manipulate the genre.

The critics' major objection to *El amo del mundo*, however, had less to do with its technical defects than it did with its feminist theme, which was largely misunderstood in the reviews that came out in the newspapers the next day. According to the critic writing for *La Nación*, "the play's thesis seems to be that men, with their pride and egotism, are solely to blame for the suffering to which women are condemned, [for they are] treated harshly when they have the sincerity to confess the truth of their situation and of their sad destiny."[1] Ironically enough, Alfonsina's thesis was exactly the opposite, for the main point of her play was to prove that women did not have to depend on men for their happiness. Márgara, the protagonist of the play, is being courted by Claudio, a rather jaded older man who had grown tired of living alone and who sees in her an experienced, educated, intelligent woman who would undoubtedly be a very suitable companion for him. Márgara, however, has seen through Claudio's pretensions, and she decides to prove to him that his so-called love is not really quite as strong and pure as he would have her believe. She tells him quite bluntly that the young boy living with her is her illegitimate son, and just as she expected, the horrified Claudio quickly retracts his marriage proposal. He is even more astonished when Márgara refuses his tentative offer to forgive her for what she has done, nor can he understand her when she claims that she is the one who has triumphed in this situation. As far as Claudio is concerned, he had the upper hand in the whole matter, for he has made all the decisions: he proposed to her, he judged her, he changed his mind, and he turned her down. But Márgara is the real winner because she made a mockery of his love, proving that it was not love but just an illusion based on his very obvious egocentricity. She had never aspired for one moment to become his wife, but had contented herself quite simply with showing him up for what he really was.

The critics of 1927 were obviously confused about this issue. They believed, perhaps because they were men, that Márgara had set her hopes on becoming a nice, middle-class woman married to a respectable man. Her plans had failed, they thought, because the man she loved had discovered just in time that she was a "fallen woman," so it appeared to them that her honesty had not paid. But Claudio had not in any way "condemned" Márgara to suffer. Quite the contrary—he became his own victim because he allowed his pride and egotism to guide him into marrying Zarcillo, a frivolous and deceit-

ful young girl. It was entirely foreseeable that Zarcillo, whom
Claudio thought was deliciously chaste, was in reality every bit as
experienced as he was. She was a sort of prototype of the liberated
woman who saw herself as being free to do what she liked, yet was
incapable of feeling anything or of understanding her own acts. She
brings to mind another character in a short story that Alfonsina
published the previous year. This other character, Cuca, was made
of sawdust, but her condition went unnoticed by the real women
with whom she spent her time in pursuit of the most extraordinarily
trivial goals.[2] Alfonsina obviously created characters like Cuca or
Zarcillo to illustrate the extremely insubstantial lives that most of
the women of her day were leading. "In my play," she explained, "I
wanted to show up frivolous women for what they really are, full of
little tricks that actually muddy them, but with a mud that is overlooked and tolerated. Most men do not even see it at all, but when
they do, it seems to act almost as a stimulus to their senses."[3]

If women learned to use clever tricks to trap unwary men, it was
because men seemed to want it that way, and they were often
charmed and delighted by these feminine wiles. This is why Claudio
was very disillusioned when Márgara refused to play the role of the
excitingly deceitful woman: "You lacked the ability and the tact to
deceive me," he complained. "You did not know how to smooth
things over, you would not gild the lily for me. My disenchantment
stems more from your attitude than from the deed itself [the illegitimate child]."[4] He insisted on living a life of tricks and illusions,
and in this way he would create his own hell, a fact so obvious that
even the maid-servant commented in the third act that nothing good
was to come of their union (p. 25). Alfonsina is telling us that men
and women who live on such a superficial level deserve each other.

But that is not the way the critics in 1927 interpreted her message, to her great surprise. In one of the articles she wrote in defense of her play she cited a journalist who claimed that "the critics
in Buenos Aires saw an arbitrary limitation in her theme, and they
felt she showed exaggerated prejudice when she divided up the
vices and virtues between the two sexes. This is why they did not
formulate a very favorable judgment."[5] Evidently the critics felt that
the women had a corner on all the virtues the author had dealt out to
her characters, yet there is little doubt that Zarcillo was a close
match for Claudio when it came to vices. Like the men Alfonsina
described in her play, the critics themselves seemed to tolerate and

overlook Zarcillo's "charming" deceptions. The playwright's intention, however, was to compare and contrast Zarcillo's and Márgara's very different viewpoints in order to show in what way the relationship between the sexes was weakened by the trivial games that are so often played, especially during courtship. In fact, Alfonsina had originally intended to call her play *Dos mujeres (Two Women)*, but the title had already been used by somebody else, so the producer decided to call it *El amo del mundo. (The Master of the World)*. It was an unfortunate choice of titles because it only contributed to the general tendency to place the emphasis on the male protagonist instead of seeing the play as being an attempt to describe the false values commonly held by both men and women. "When I went out into the world and observed things with my own eyes," explained Alfonsina, "not with the limitations imposed on my sex, but as a person who can forget about such things . . . I found that men and women had assumed battle positions. The former were hoping to obtain some pleasurable tidbits, while the latter were trying to find someone to feed them. I found that, on a global scale, women possess as many virtues and defects as men, but that they are each of a different type."[6] These words are hardly those of a woman who had been embittered by men, or who was prejudiced in favor of the female sex.

These observations led her to some very logical conclusions. She had no choice but to attack the sacred cow of any conservative and traditional culture like her own: the institution of marriage. Strangely enough, the critics never made any comments at all about this. It is possible that this part of the play was cut out of the script used for the actual performance—one line was deleted because the female lead refused to utter the word "celestina" ("go-between")— but there is now no way of knowing just what lines were censored. However, in spite of this otherwise incomprehensible silence on the part of the critics, the scene dealing with the subject of marriage is the most original and dramatic moment of the play. In this scene Márgara explains to the very deflated Claudio that the relationship between a woman and her lover tends to be much more honest and disinterested than that of a married couple. Whereas a man can accept almost any woman as his mistress, he generally feels that few women would deserve to become his wife. But Márgara sees things from an opposite viewpoint, and she tells Claudio that she did not marry the father of her child because her relationship with him

meant too much to her, and she was afraid to destroy it by trying to
make it fit into a conventional mold. Claudio is not convinced,
however, and he accuses her of being a wounded creature who is
attempting to turn her very wounds into a form of strength. Márgara
answers him passionately: "You are wrong. I am much more than a
woman: I am a human being. And beside you, since I do not need
you, I am a free person. And do you know why I am free? It is
because I do not feel personally offended by an act of love. I see you
as an equal. I speak to you as an equal. I judge you as an equal
(p. 22)."

"I am much more than a woman: I am a human being." With
these words Alfonsina proved herself to be fifty years ahead of her
time. She had the extraordinary strength and courage to speak her
mind at a time when social rules were very rigid, and women from
"good families" simply did not voice such revolutionary ideas, nor
could they permit themselves the luxury of behaving in an unconventional way. Once, for example, when Alfonsina was teaching at
the Escuela Normal de Lenguas Vivas, she decided to bob her hair.
When the headmistress saw her, she was so distressed that she
made her wear a false bun.[7] Even with her false bun Alfonsina could
not be silenced, and the consequences were often very disagree-
able. Claudio believed, just as many men must have believed at the
time, that an intelligent woman is "a hybrid thing, that has neither
the reckless audacity of a man nor the modesty and coquettishness
of a woman, which are their strongest weapons. Of what use is it for
her to philosophize? It barely helps her to break her moral ties. . . .
She cannot be free except by denying love, because she
philosophizes, but Nature burdens her with a child, and then what
is the use of talking? Then comes what nobody can understand in a
free woman, and that is when she hides from her own child the fact
that she is his mother. She denies him the right to call her by her
name" (p. 23). Claudio has put his finger in the wound, and for the
first time he gives Márgara something serious to think about.

From that moment on Márgara begins to delve more deeply into
her ideas about freedom. Until then her opinions had been based
mainly on her reactions to a society she found unacceptable, but she
had not yet begun to form a philosophy of her own. In spite of all her
brave words, she herself was living according to society's hypocritical rules when she hid from her son the fact that she was his mother.
She thought she was doing it for his own good, to protect him from

the hostility of others, but Claudio helped her to understand that there was no room for halfway measures in her life. She decided to surrender herself completely to the freedom she had chosen, and to take her son with her on this voyage of experimentation and discovery. She had learned that the fundamental thing in the life of any human being, man or woman, was to establish a profound and loving relationship with another person. Márgara is finally able to bring this about at the end of the play when she confesses to her son that she is his mother. She at last found the courage she needed to get rid of all the falseness and hypocrisy which had existed in the only relationship that was really important to her. She had grown emotionally, like the characters in one of her pyrotechnical farces who, at the end of the play, found that they could no longer fit back into the book from which they had emerged.[8]

When the curtain fell after the first performance the audience applauded and called for the author. The applause on that opening night no doubt reflected Alfonsina's enormous popularity with the public, who read and admired her well-known collections of poetry. Perhaps they also applauded because they realized somehow that they had just seen a very uncommon play, but judging from the commentaries that were written later, nobody really grasped the meaning of the passionate speeches they had heard. This very worthy play has been largely forgotten today, in part because Alfonsina's biographers and critics have tended to repeat the negative opinions that were expressed in the reviews that came out in 1927. The time for a reevaluation is long overdue.[9]

II   La técnica de Mister Dougall (Mister Dougall's Technique)

Alfonsina started writing this play shortly after completing *El amo del mundo*,[10] but it was never performed or published.[11] The play, which was originally called *La borrachera de Mister Dougall* (Mister Dougall's Drunken Spree),[12] was written expressly for Tita Merello, who has since become a well-known actress in Argentina. Alfonsina imagined her as being the perfect one to play the female lead, but apparently the part did not appeal to her, so Alfonsina must have packed the play away for a while. In April, 1931, she turned her attention to it again and gave it the final touches,[13] but by August of the same year it had already been rejected by two producers. "*La técnica de Mister Dougall* [as she decided to call it] has come up against a brick wall twice now," she explained in an interview. "At

first I offered it to my nice friend Carcavallo, but he would not even
deign to read it because, since it was mine, he assumed that it would
be too intellectual for his theater. So then I gave it to Areta, but he
told me that it was too refined for the national theater, for in this
time of crisis what was needed were political plays or else lavish
spectacles."[14] She must have become discouraged after these three
failures to interest people in *Dougall*, and from then on she concentrated mainly on writing plays for her student productions in the
Lavarden Theater where she taught acting.

It is entirely possible that the producers were unwilling to take a
chance on her after observing how her first play had closed so soon
after opening night, but the irony is that *Dougall* was actually a
better play in terms of theatrical technique. Although the play's
thesis was similar to that of *El amo del mundo,* it was presented
indirectly to the audience through the action of the characters rather
than through dialogues which directly expressed the playwright's
point of view. Both plays describe the difficulties encountered by
men and women when their relationship to one another is based on
false values. The two works also contrast and compare the roles that
the female characters play in regard to the male protagonist, but the
two women in *Dougall* have completely lost the self-consciousness
of their counterparts in *El amo del mundo.* They never discuss their
attitudes about marriage and men, nor do they use the stage as a
place to debate social injustices toward women. Instead, the action
speaks for itself as the characters respond in their different ways to
the various situations.

The main conflict centers around the drinking habits of Mr.
Dougall, who is a handsome, enterprising, and very successful
owner of a whiskey distillery. His position requires that he assidu-
ously taste a large number of samples of his product, so by the end of
each day he greets his new criolla bride in a state of happy but
strictly controlled inebriation, in perfect accordance with his British
upbringing. Even though he executes some astonishing feats of
mental arithmetic in order to prove to his wife that the alcohol has
not affected his mind, she is neither impressed nor amused by his
performance and she demands that he give up his job immediately.
He refuses to comply, she nags, he grows tired of her in-laws, she
makes scenes, and finally he ends up in the arms of his secretary,
who knew all along how to attract him by flattering him and pretending to be all sweetness and innocence. His wife walks in just as

they are embracing, whereupon she declares that she intends to leave him. Once again the designing woman wins the questionable reward of marrying a well-heeled but superficial man, while the woman who had the courage to speak her mind ends up with her freedom and with her dignity intact.

Except for this central thesis, however, the two plays differ from each other in almost every way. Although Alfonsina succeeded this time in expressing herself through the interaction of her characters rather than stating her ideas through direct debate on the stage, this fundamental improvement in her technique led to a new defect that was not present in her first play. Whereas in *El amo del mundo* the characters tended to sit around discussing theories, in *Dougall* they were forced by the action to move about a great deal more, as each character developed his particular relationship with the others. As a result, Alfonsina resorted to some rather amateurish tactics when it came time to move her characters: the servant had to be sent on an unnecessary errand, the sister had a sudden yearning for some tea and had to retire to the kitchen to steep it, and two characters had to be called to the balcony to witness a totally irrelevant car accident in the street below. The defect of irrelevance became particularly apparent when for some unknown reason the playwright found it necessary to make the sister a hemiplegiac who had been run over by a streetcar.

In general, however, the technical improvements far outweigh the defects in this second play, and there is every reason to believe that it would have met with considerable success if it had been produced. This is not to say that the content itself was in any way superior to that of *El amo del mundo*. On the contrary, Alfonsina was always at her best when she had the freedom to express herself directly, without having to work around the restrictions imposed by the various literary genres. She had been criticized severely when she used poetry for outlining her ideas about social and sexual injustices,[15] and *El amo del mundo* failed partly because the characters untheatrically explained the playwright's opinions on the stage, so in *Dougall* she concentrated on getting her message across indirectly through the action of the characters. As a result, *Dougall* succeeded technically where *El amo del mundo* failed, although the latter was unquestionably more effective in communicating the author's specific ideas. The truth is that Alfonsina was better at writing essays than plays. Had she persevered in writing for the theater, however, she might have had to find some way of combining her talent for nonfictional prose with the dialogue form, as George Bernard Shaw did, for example, in the prologues to his plays.

There were nevertheless many felicitous moments in *La técnica de Mister Dougall*, and the protagonist would no doubt have appealed greatly to the audience in Buenos Aires in the late twenties or early thirties. The technique mentioned in the title referred to Dougall's self-vaunted ability to carry on his business affairs on a grand scale, thanks to his knowledge of the newest commercial and industrial methods. In some ways he was a stereotype of the typical British businessman who had gone to Argentina to make a fortune—he was totally involved in his search for material success, he was self-loving but also attracted to the fiery women of the "inferior races," he showed considerable disdain for the citizens of his host country, and he kept everybody at arm's length by perpetually playing the role of the perfect gentleman. Alfonsina's audience would have enjoyed having a good laugh at the foreigner who remained in haughty isolation while at the same time benefitting from the many opportunities he found in his adopted country. Argentinians at that time had become fed up with British and American business concerns which they felt were making unfair profits at their expense. It was only ten years later that Juan Perón won great acclaim and public support when he promised to rid his country of unwelcome foreign interests.[16]

But Dougall, after all, was the male lead, and Alfonsina could hardly afford to paint him all black, so she presented him with some superficially redeeming features: he was young, he was handsome, and, of course, he had plenty of pesos which he handed around with expansive generosity. He attracted the women in his life by the very fact that he was a foreigner who amused them without his knowing quite why. His apparently ardent passion, for example, was constantly being interrupted by his irrepressible urge to translate his terms of endearment into English because that way they sounded more significant to him, even though the translation added nothing to the understanding of his hispanophone beloveds: "Linda mariposita, 'butterfly' en inglés, venga Ud. aquí!" (Act Three). Dougall, however, was not unlike Claudio, the protagonist of *El amo del mundo*, in that he was also essentially unaware that women existed as human beings and not just as playthings suitable only for giving pleasure or being pampered. This unfortunate failing on the part of Dougall was made evident in the last act when he began to woo his secretary with exactly the same words he had used in the first act to win and wed his wife. The business of love was a mere convenience for both Dougall and Claudio, who saw women as charming creatures whose only role was to sweeten their lives and flatter their egos.

This male viewpoint, and in those days men were by no means ashamed to admit such attitudes, was presented far more gracefully in *Dougall* than in *El amo del mundo*. There was considerable humor in Dougall's self-satisfaction, and his alcoholism was never overdone. His secretary craftily shared his great interest in whiskey, and as a reward for her appreciation he presented her with one of his prize bottles, which she happily tippled as she typed. His wife, instead of making speeches about male chauvinism, darkly threatened to leave his house stark naked because she wanted to prove to him that she was an independent woman and did not need the clothes he gave her, or any of the other material benefits he provided, for that matter. Although in some ways she seemed to fit the stereotype of the Latin firecracker, her proud superiority was not irritating, as it occasionally was in the case of Márgara. Technically this is because Alfonsina allowed Márgara to speak as though she were reciting one of her own essays on injustice, so although her words were incisive and intelligent, her cool-headed logic gained her very little sympathy as a character. Dougall's wife, on the other hand, was all emotion and reaction, so she came across as a vital, courageous woman, albeit overly demanding. Had she been any older she would have come close to being a shrew, but her very youth and frankness inspired a feeling of benevolence. Like Márgara, however, she was at a technical disadvantage in that she was forced to play straightman to her husband and brother, who were in a more or less perpetual state of inebriation. Dougall was always upstaging her because he was the *enfant terrible* who did exactly as he pleased and who got all the laughs. Her role would not have been particularly attractive to a prima donna because Dougall would have no doubt stolen the show, and this may very well account for why Tita Merello turned down the part.

In spite of these defects, *La técnica de Mister Dougall* is better theater than *El amo del mundo*. The injustices inherent in the traditional relationship between men and women are treated with humorous irony in *Dougall*, instead of with the anguished intensity of *El amo*. Although the male protagonists of both plays have an inflated ego, the self-image that Dougall projects is a satire of the male chauvinist and the typical business entrepreneur, whereas Claudio is less appealing because he presents a more realistic picture of a man who takes his superiority for granted. Dougall sees himself as an anonymous hero (a term which he translates into English to impress his secretary) whose chivalric strength lies in his ability to challenge and subdue the dragon of modern technology, which he uses to produce better whiskey at lower prices. Dougall would succeed on the stage because he is a literary character, larger than life, but Claudio failed because he was too much like the average man in the street, devoid of any features that could elicit either pity, fear, or laughter from the audience. The characters in *La técnica de Mister Dougall* come to life and capture the attention. It is a shame that this play has never been produced or published.

III   *Dos farsas pirotécnicas (Two Pyrotechnical Farces)*

By 1931 Alfonsina had completed two more plays which were published in book form the following year.[17] The first, a full-length play called *Cimbelina en 1900 y pico (Cymbeline in 1900 Or So)*,[18] is a superficial farce which bases its plot on the main action of Shakespeare's *Cymbeline*. In her prologue Alfonsina has the characters step out of a giant book representing Shakespeare's play, whereupon they explain to the audience who they are and what happened to them in the original work. The main character is Imógena, daughter of Cimbelina and wife of Póstumo, a poor gentleman. Her father, the king, is enraged by her marriage to a commoner, so he sends Póstumo into exile. There he meets Joáquimo, who feels intrigued and challenged by his descriptions of his wife's incomparable beauty and virtue. Joáquimo makes a bet with Póstumo that he can seduce her, but he fails. In order to save his self-respect he pretends that his mission was successful, and the horrified Póstumo vows to kill Imógena. Through a series of events his wife's innocence is finally established, and all is well that ends well.

The characters then pass through a sort of time screen located at stage center, and proceed to act out the situation all over again, but this time the action takes place in 1900 or so. Whereas Shakespeare used this thin plot as a framework for his commentaries on life and human nature, Alfonsina uses the outline primarily as a means of comparing contemporary customs with those described in the original *Cymbeline*. The results are farcical, which is what the author intended, but this play is perhaps the least interesting of her repertory.

The modern counterparts to Shakespeare's characters are insipid stereotypes: King Cymbeline becomes a weak-kneed minister of state who has no authority in his family, his wife is a shrew, Imógena is a spoiled and rather silly young woman, Póstumo is a poor lawyer who fancies himself a revolutionary out to save the world, and Joáquimo is a typical Don Juan. These characters are essentially two-dimensional, and consequently the author had to depend on the plot to motivate them, rather than establishing motivation through the interaction of one personality with another. The characters understandably behave in an almost mechanical fashion, which is perfectly allowable in a farce, but there is not enough plot to make up for their lack of depth. Alfonsina lifted only the main action from Shakespeare's play, leaving the characters with no particular motivation and a good deal of time on their hands. As a result she was forced to fill all the gaps as best she could with whatever commentary came to mind. On at least three occasions she was totally unable to come up with some plausible action to take the place of the subplot which she had decided to leave out of her rendition of Shakespeare's *Cymbeline*: in the fifth act she had the maid recount not one but two very lengthy stories to Imógena, who was waiting for Joáquimo to come to a tryst. Later on in the same act she had the telephone ring, which gave the protagonist a chance to pass the time and amuse the audience by playing cat and mouse with somebody who had evidently dialed the wrong number. In the sixth act she found herself at such a complete loss for filler material that she simply had a stagehand appear and explain to the audience that the author needed some extra time to let the main characters accomplish their business. He merely stood around on the stage making small talk until it was time for the other characters to return, and then he climbed back down into the orchestra.

Alfonsina tried hard to bring the play to life through various devices. One of her main techniques was to superimpose new times over old, an idea that had considerable potential for appealing to the audience, given the tendency of many people either to idealize the past or else to laugh at it, but she did not make the most of the situation. She seemed content to substitute contemporary objects

for those that served in Shakespeare's play, as for example when
Imógena gives the parting Póstumo her Gillette razor as a token of
her esteem. Modern-day instruments also serve as plot modifiers, as
when Imógena takes a hydroplane to Póstumo's place of exile in
order to warn him ahead of time that Joáquimo is planning to deceive him. One of her more controversial devices was the sudden
apparition at stage left of a "huge, grotesque hand, sustained by an
unlikely looking sleeve" (p. 40), which gives the leading lady a
revolver with which to threaten her importunate suitor. But of all
the techniques and devices Alfonsina used in this farce, perhaps the
least successful was the rather too obvious symbolism she created in
an attempt to delineate better the personality of her characters.
Póstumo, the self-styled revolutionary in 1900 or so, constantly
hammers away at a large globe of the world in a vain attempt to "fix"
it. Imógena does what she can to help him by caressing the globe
and talking to it soothingly, but neither the aggressive male approach nor the loving female attitude do much in the way of
improving the sad condition of the world. What is worse, Póstumo's
leftist tendencies are complemented by the fact that Imógena is
left-handed, a point the author makes several times. As for the
minister of state, he spends his time trying to compensate for his
lack of authority by blowing on the sails of a toy boat which he calls
his "ship of state" (p. 23). His wife emphasizes her manipulative
tendencies by dancing a marionette on the table.

Ironically, this farce was very well received by the critics. Their
positive reviews may have been colored by the fact that the play was
produced in homage to Alfonsina two months after her suicide;
nevertheless the commentaries showed a true appreciation for this
insubstantial piece of entertainment. *La Nación* praised it as being
an "intellectual satire of modern customs, touching on a great vari-
ety of topics,"[19] *Crítica* was impressed by her use of symbolism,[20]
La Prensa saw in it "the characteristic intelligence and passion of the
author,"[21] *La Razón* felt the play revealed the author's "ductile
talent," which showed her to be capable of tackling "the most
difficult themes and states of being,"[22] and *El Mundo* went so far as
to compare her favorably with Shaw.[23] It would appear that Alfonsina had finally succeeded in giving the public and the critics a
product that they found considerably more appealing than her first
efforts, but she bought her success at the expense of the play's
potential merit. *El amo del mundo* had been criticized for being too

"serious" and too "intellectual," so she evidently decided to pander to public opinion by leaving such ingredients out of *Cymbeline*. As a result, her play has neither the moral commentary of good satire, nor the wit and profundity of comedy, nor even the technical brilliance of first-rate slapstick. There are occasional touches of whimsy, such as when the characters discover at the end of the play that they can no longer fit back into the book from which they had emerged in the beginning because they had grown "psychically," but one is hard-pressed to understand in what way they had actually matured. It is unfortunate, in a way, that she chose Shakespeare as her model because any comparison on any level to the original only makes the defects in this rendition the more evident.

The second of the two so-called pyrotechnical farces, *Polixena y la cocinerita (Polixena and the Little Cook)*, is a one-act play with a short epilogue. The action takes place in an imaginatively stylized kitchen, where the little cook is busily reading Euripides while she is washing the dishes. In case any questions should arise in the minds of the spectators as to the likelihood of a cook's being interested in classical Greek literature, the author had her protagonist tell her friend the maid that she is really a well-educated young lady who decided to escape from the suffocating atmosphere of her family and go forth to explore the world. The idea has interesting potential, but unfortunately it came to nothing. The whole situation was created only to explain the presence of Euripides in the kitchen where Alfonsina located him because she had decided that her play was to be a farce. The cook is particularly attracted by Polixena in Euripides' tragedy *Hecuba,* for she was a model of heroism and resignation in the way she accepted the Achaean's decision to sacrifice her on Achilles' tomb after the fall of Troy. The death of the little cook at the end of the act comes as no surprise, therefore, after the obvious foreshadowing which emerges from the comparison between the two women. What does come as a shock, however, is the complete inappropriateness of the author's attempt to establish parallels between the protagonist of her farce and the heroine of Euripides' tragedy.

In Alfonsina's play, the cook is constantly being harassed by the young master of the house, who levels a good number of insults at her for not having taken him up on his proposal to make love with him. The maid tries to cheer up her friend the cook when she sees how miserable she feels, by reminding her of Polixena's nobility and courage in the face of adversity. Suddenly the cook, "with a shout of triumphant joy, heroic, with increasing exaltation" (p. 145) decides to act out Polixena's death for the maid. She gathers together a group of diverse kitchen utensils to represent Achilles' tomb, and she lines up a pile of cabbages to depict the Achaean soldiers. She then recites eleven pages written in free verse describing Polixena's pitiful circumstances, at the end of which she takes a kitchen knife, and pretending to be her own executioner, she plunges the weapon into herself and falls over dead. The maid runs off the stage screaming for help as the curtain falls. In the epilogue, which takes place in Hades, Euripides is told by a giant fish that his tragedy has been profaned by a modern-day Argentine poet by the name of Alfonsina Storni. His dead spirit is so horrified at the news that it commits suicide by diving into the open mouth of the fish.

Alfonsina's underlying intentions are quite clear: she had hoped to create a character who shared Polixena's courage in accepting death rather than living in slavery, even though slavery, in the little cook's case, was symbolized merely by her being subjected to the vulgarity of a hopelessly mediocre male. There was such a vast discrepancy, however, between the quality of the two protagonists and their situations that the results proved not to be what Alfonsina had expected. One of the greatest risks that a playwright takes in composing a farce is that of inspiring the audience or reader to laugh at the play itself instead of laughing at what it proposes to satirize. No doubt Alfonsina underestimated the problems involved in writing a farce, for *Polixena y la cocinerita* is unquestionably her least successful play. Like its sister farce, *Cimbelina en 1900 y pico*, it was never produced during her lifetime. After her suicide, however, it was given one reading in homage to her in the Teatro Intimo of La Peña, a distinguished literary circle to which she belonged for many years.

It is ironic that each play she wrote turned out to be worse than the one before, and even more ironic that the critics should have panned *El amo del mundo*, her first and best play in terms of its content, while praising *Cimbelina*, one of her last and greatest failures. The irony here does not imply that the situation is in any way untrue to life—it is only a shame that Alfonsina should have put so much faith in the opinion of others when it came to writing plays. Her first play was the only one that had any real substance. *Dougall* had considerably less depth but was better theater. One might have hoped that at this juncture she could have come up with the right combination on her third try, but instead she sacrificed even the pretense of sound content in the pyrotechnical farces, for she seemed quite satisfied to give the audience a production that was all veneer. Unfortunately the fireworks she had envisioned in the title simply never went off.

IV *Teatro infantil (Plays for Children)*

In 1921 Alfonsina was given a position as drama instructor in the Lavarden Theater for children. Every Sunday her pupils were expected to give public performances in the parks and squares of Buenos Aires, for the entertainment of anyone who happened to be out for a walk. The roving players would carry with them their props and costumes, while Alfonsina called together the Sunday strollers and generally supervised the day's production. She wrote most of the plays herself, in great haste, snatching time whenever she could between her other infinite duties as teacher, mother, poet, and theatrical director.[24] The plays she wrote for the children were certainly not as self-conscious as the ones she wrote for the general public because she had no need to worry about either the critics' opinions or the in-fighting that is so common among professionals. And yet in spite of the freedom from critical scrutiny that she enjoyed in this genre, the results are often disappointing. Except for occasional touches of lyricism and some imaginative moments, these plays indicate that their author was hurried and careless, and not as original as she might have been, perhaps, if she had been working under less pressure.

The most obvious example of her lack of originality is found in her best-known children's play, *Blanco . . . negro . . . blanco (White . . . Black . . . White)*,[25] which she lifted almost entirely from Leopoldo Lugones' pantomime, "El Pierrot negro" ("Black Pierrot"), first published in 1909 in his *Lunario sentimental (Sentimental Journey to the Moon)*. One must resist the temptation, of course, to judge her children's plays from the same perspective as one views the rest of her literary creations, for she clearly had no intention of writing for posterity when she put together something for her pupils to perform in the park. One cannot, then, demand originality or excellence from a writer who is composing plays on the side, so to speak, but one must also beware of giving Alfonsina too much credit for *Blanco . . . negro . . . blanco*, an error into which Arturo Capdevila fell in his otherwise sensitive comparison between Lugones' pantomime and Alfonsina's copy.[26] In Lugones' version, Colombine and Harlequin constantly played cruel jokes on the lovelorn Pierrot, who nevertheless followed them around faithfully so as not to lose sight of his beloved Colombine. At one point they pulled a ladder away, causing Pierrot to fall headlong into a vat of black dye. There seemed to be no way of getting rid of it, so in desperation he went to an alchemist and explained to him that Colombine would never love him as long as he remained black. At first the alchemist tried to cure him by offering him a new love, but when that failed, he decided to send Pierrot to the moon, the empire of whiteness. Pierrot flew there on a broom provided by the alchemist, but to his dismay he found that he was still black, and that the moon was nothing but an arid desert. His loneliness was accentuated by the terrible silence that surrounded him, but suddenly it was broken by Colombine's laughter. When Pierrot looked toward the earth through his telescope, he saw Colombine dancing slowly and snugly in Harlequin's arms. The sight of this caused him such despair that he jumped off the moon, and landed at Colombine's feet. The loud crash scared everybody away. But Colombine, who thought Pierrot was dead, threw herself on his body, weeping. Her love and concern soon revived him, and they embraced each other with joy and relief. Harlequin came back onto the scene and reproached Colombine for her behavior, but she made it clear to him that she no longer loved him because he had run away like a coward, whereas Pierrot had had the courage to go to the moon and back, all for her sake. In answer to his companions' questions, Pierrot explained that the clouds washed him clean again on his way back to earth. Then he tried to give Colombine a handful of diamonds that he had brought back from the moon, but she disdainfully threw them behind her, and kissed him while the others scrambled for the precious stones.

Alfonsina's version, written in verse, is almost exactly the same as that of Lugones, except that Harlequin is omitted altogether. As a result, Colombine's motive for no longer loving Pierrot is based entirely on the fact that he has accidentally become black, and her love is rekindled not because he proved to be more courageous than his rival, but because he had managed to whiten himself again. This necessarily makes Alfonsina's Colombine a more superficial character than that of Lugones, but the inherent symbolism of the white, black, white theme rescues both characters from the triviality with which they have always been treated in literary tradition. Capdevila rightly sees this theme as one that lends itself to many interpretations. According to his point of view, Pierrot's blackness symbolizes man in his fallen state, and his trip to the moon represents man's anxious desire to return to his original purity and innocence.[27] He might well have gone on to say that Pierrot's success was based on his unshakeable love, a factor which cannot be overlooked in an account of this kind. The implications here are almost infinite, and one must resist the temptation to analyze a story that Alfonsina did not create herself. The important thing is that it obviously appealed to her, and the fact that she based her play on it tells us something about the author herself. Capdevila believes that this play is Alfonsina's most transcendental work,[28] and it is difficult to prove him wrong. One thinks immediately of the corpus of poetry as being the obvious place to find other themes touching on the universal, but although one can easily remember similar motifs (the longing for perfection, the love that stops at nothing, the restless search for a solution to her unhappiness), it would perhaps be a far harder task to discover what could be called a transcendental quality in her poetry. It is disappointing to have to admit that her most transcendental work, to use Capdevila's words again, was one so closely based on the creation of another poet.

Another motif that appears in the children's plays is the defense of freedom. The victims in need of liberation are twice portrayed as birds, as in the case of *Pedro y Pedrito* and *El dios de los pájaros (The God of the Birds)*. In the first play two parrots are set free from their cage by their friend the mouse, and thus delivered from their wicked owners. In the second play some children who enjoy shooting birds with their slingshots are taught a lesson by the bird-god, who locks them up in a cage until they repent. One is inevitably reminded of Alfonsina's well-known poem entitled *Hombre pequeñito (Little Man)*,[29] in which the poet, trapped by the mediocrity of an uninspiring love affair, asks to be let out of her cage. In both these plays the value of the individual, above all the helpless individual, is protected and upheld.

The first of the two plays is an occasionally humorous, black-and-white melodrama of villains and victims. The second, however, may very well be her best children's play. Since the "villains" this time are themselves children, the author paints them in various

shades of gray instead of making them all black, and they emerge as
a group of reasonably innocent little people with failings that are all
too human. When two of their companions are carried off by the
bird-god for threatening to shoot a bird they heard singing in a tree,
the rest of the group decides to rescue them in spite of the bitterly
cold weather in the mountains. They brave the weather and the
dangerous conditions for three days, complaining very little about
hunger and fear. By the time they make it to the top of the moun-
tain, they have achieved a certain measure of true heroism. Meanwhile, in his fantasy-land palace, the bird-god orders his subordi-
nates to treat the two little prisoners firmly but kindly. He is careful
to make sure that the jailers understand that the only way to teach
the children their lesson is to make them change places with the
birds they had intended to kill. "I don't want them to hate the god of
the birds, but I do want them to know how hard it is to be locked up
in a cage . . . [Treat them] with the pleasant affability with which
people treat their pet canaries."[30]
    The children face their ordeal bravely and refuse to cry, but they
are not quick to grasp the point of the exercise because they are
convinced that humans are worth more than birds. They conclude,
therefore, that it is far more unjust for the birds to put them in a
cage than it is for people to do the same to birds. Just then the
rescue party comes bursting in, and the children are reunited. The
leader starts negotiations with the bird-god, explaining to him that
the prisoners' parents are undoubtedly suffering from terrible anxiety about their absent children. Two of the party step forward and
ask to be substituted for the original pair, for they are orphans and
can afford to disappear without upsetting anybody. The bird-god is
impressed by the children's courage, but he does not miss the opportunity of leading them toward a better understanding of the
obvious implications of their role-reversal. Finally the full meaning
of their experience dawns on the children, and they promise to
adopt a more humane attitude toward birds. The bird-god is delighted at their new insight and sets them free at once. "I am not
cruel," he tells them, "I want to be fair. You behaved like true
men. . . . I am sure that you will keep your promise."[31] The bird-
god has achieved his goal; it is love, not force, that wins the day, and
both the birds and the children have a new respect for one another.
    This all-but-forgotten children's play takes on new importance
when judged in the light of the many statements Alfonsina made

about the need to liberate women, and it would not be far-fetched to seek parallels between the birds and the children, and between the women and the men of Buenos Aires in her day. The children behaved like the men who inspired both love and exasperation in the author: they were courageous, determined, and loyal, but at the same time they were strangely blind to the feelings of women, whom they hurt partly because they considered them to be inferior creatures. Even when they dealt with them as kindly as possible, it was still "with the pleasant affability with which people treat their pet canaries." One of the key statements in the play is expressed by the child who says that the birds are behaving unjustly toward them in making them prisoners, because humans are more important than birds.[32] It is significant here that this opinion blocks any possibility of change or insight on his part. It is not until the full effects of the role-reversal are felt by the children that they can behave like "true men," and make a promise which the bird-god knows they will keep. Of interest, too, is the fact that *El dios de los pájaros* is the only work in Alfonsina's repertory in which two opposing factions finally settle their differences. In *El amo del mundo*, Márgara was unable to break through Claudio's egocentricity, and the same was true of Mr. Dougall's wife in the author's second play. Alfonsina's poetry and essays give evidence of both hope and despair when she analyzes human relationships, but there are no triumphs like the one depicted in *El dios de los pájaros*. Perhaps only in a world of fantasy is it possible to create a situation in which people can experience spiritual growth and deepen their understanding of others by literally changing places with those whom they initially scorned or ignored. Love can achieve this too, of course, but it fails to do so in any of Alfonsina's other works. One is left with the feeling that she has touched on a major theme in this children's play, and one can only regret that she never developed it further in her other literary efforts.

Alfonsina uses the same motif, the desire for freedom, once again in another children's play called *Los degolladores de estatuas (The Beheaders of Statues)*, but this time she resolves the conflict in quite a different way. The action takes place in a house in a wealthy neighborhood, and as the curtain rises the members of the household are getting ready to go shopping. As soon as they leave, the dolls come to life and complain about the way they are treated by their young owners. Each one dreams of what he would do if he were free until finally they decide to wage a revolution against their masters. One of the little girl dolls convinces the others to avoid bloodshed, however, and after some discussion they all agree to vent their pent-up rage on the statues whom they gleefully behead. At this point the family members return, take one look at the mutilated statues, and call the police. When they leave the room, the dolls quickly replace the heads, so that when the police arrive they think that the family is playing a practical joke on them. The family and the police level all sorts of bitter accusations at one another, until finally nobody is on speaking terms with anybody else. The dolls all have a good laugh and congratulate themselves for so successfully getting their revenge on their owners. One can imagine that this play must have delighted Alfonsina's young actors, and it must have been popular with the Sunday afternoon strollers.

The above play completes the collection of those that have been published. Three others are still available in manuscript form in the archives of the Lavarden Theater in Buenos Aires. Two of them, *La sirvienta moderna (The Modern Servant)* and *La sirvienta mecánica (The Mechanical Servant)*, are of interest for the social commentary that Alfonsina makes on the subject of domestic service. In the first play, a servant manages to convince the family for whom she works to go along with her scheme of mutual help and cooperation in running the household and completing the chores. In the second, a family becomes disgusted with the ineptitude of their maid, and replaces her with a robot, only to find that her mechanical counterpart is just as inefficient as she was. Alfonsina effectively satirizes the pompous attitudes and questionable values of the bourgeoisie, especially where domestic service is concerned, and one must once again admire her courage in attacking this institution which served the interests of so many "nice" families. It is not surprising that these two plays were omitted from the published collection whose limited first edition was printed especially for presentation to members of the higher strata of Buenos Aires society. As for the third play, *Los cazadores de fieras (The Big Game Hunters)*, this was rightly left out of the published collection, for it is based entirely on an infantile practical joke which is of no interest at all.

V Intermedio poético (Poetic Interlude)

Before closing this section on Alfonsina's theatrical compositions, brief mention should be made of the "Poetic Interlude" she wrote for Carlos Cucullu's two-act drama entitled *Judith*. This short entr'acte, presented in the Teatro Colón on August 18, 1938, and published posthumously in libretto form (Buenos Aires, October, 1939), describes how the Old Testament heroine saves her city from its captors. Although Alfonsina fails to recreate the spiritual complexity of her biblical model, she does succeed in imbuing the scene with poetic descriptions and contrasts that reflect the terror and determination of a chaste young girl being led to the tent of the man she intends to murder, while all around her the night is filled with the scent of wild lilies.

CHAPTER 4

The Prose Writer

I Prose Fiction

IN 1912, when Alfonsina was twenty and had just moved to Buenos Aires, she published her first short story in *Fray Mocho*.[1] Her son was born that year, and life was by no means easy for the young unmarried mother. She was able to draw some strength from the love she felt for the father of her child, but he lived far away, so she had to learn to tap her own private resources for the energy and optimism she needed to face a disapproving world. She became a fighter at an early age. If she was criticized, she made searing retorts; if she was attacked, she promptly fought back; if she was snubbed, she discomfited the enemy with her strident laughter. This defiant attitude is clearly evident in many of her early writings, but most particularly in her prose compositions. Her first short story, "De la vida" ("About Life"), is a bitter, undisguised attack on the hypocrisy of the bourgeoisie. It describes how a pretentious housewife hires a young girl to tutor her children at an outrageously low salary, then boasts to her friends about how much she pays her, how well dressed she is, and what a distinguished family name she has. Meanwhile, to ensure that her friends never actually lay eyes on this marvel, she orders the girl, who is poorly dressed and underfed, to sneak into the house via the back door.

Four years went by before Alfonsina published anything again, then suddenly, toward the end of the year 1916, three more stories appeared in *La Nota*, a magazine to which she was to contribute the greater part of her prose fiction in the years to come. The first of these, "Una carta" ("A Letter"),[2] was written in the epistolary form, a form which appealed to her so greatly that she wrote over a third of her prose fiction in this style. These letters were generally addressed to a lover, real or imaginary, to whom she would confess her hidden feelings. They provided her an outlet for what was inevitably the other side of her proud self-sufficiency: a vulnerable sensitivity which expressed itself in terms that were often overly sentimental and self-pitying. In her second published letter, "Algunas líneas" ("A Few Lines"),[3] the writer complains to the addressee of her misery and loneliness, accentuating her unhappiness with references to their past love. There are moments, however, when the story as a whole is redeemed by certain expressions which herald the talent of the future poet. Such a moment can be found in the paragraph in which she states that she is pained by the thought that her lover is carrying on as usual, untormented by any memory of her, while she is still attached to him with bonds of fragrant jasmines.

The third story in *La Nota* that same year, "La fina crueldad" ("Refined Cruelty"),[4] is markedly different in both style and content from the first two. Even though Alfonsina liked to claim that her writing was "absolutely free of the influence of any model,"[5] the theme of this story makes it quite clear that she had nevertheless absorbed some of the literary fashions of her day. In it she describes a woman whose characteristics were far from uncommon in the literature produced during the transitional years between the waning Romantic period and the nascent Modernist movement: she is pale, cold, haughty, beautiful, an accomplished pianist and painter, profoundly dispirited, ultra-sensitive, and altogether too good for this world. Like many a Modernist fictional character, she lives in an artificial world created by the intellect, aloof from the business of everyday life and untouched by ordinary concerns. Her only contact with reality is a healthy, exuberant, earthy young girl who admires her canvases with bewildered awe and sits at her feet while she plays melancholy compositions on the piano. One day, while contemplating the youthful beauty of her sleeping friend, it occurs to her that she would be even more beautiful if she were dead. Her deep breathing would no longer disturb her features, her skin would be as pale as the moon, and her hands would acquire the translucency of mother-of-pearl. But when, later that afternoon, she again gazes at her friend gathering flowers in the sunny garden, she feels suddenly ashamed of her own refinement, and repelled by the thought of her cruel and morbid musings while the young girl was asleep. At that moment she becomes the victim of her own gray existence, for as she stands there watching her friend emanate energy, joy, enthusiasm, and love of life, her very heart is turned to earth. It is not improbable that the symbolic death of the "decadent" older woman showed that Alfonsina was now ready to align herself with those who were calling for someone to twist the neck of the swan (see early part of Chapter 2). It is possible, too, that the fact that the woman's heart turned to earth (and not to stone, for example) suggests that she yearned to share the high-spirited vitality of her friend, but that her inability to do so was responsible for her destruction. Ironically, it is destiny that practices a refined sort of cruelty on the protagonist of the story, and not the protagonist, as she herself believes, who is cruel in conjuring up a morbid picture of her sleeping friend.

Two years later, in 1918, Alfonsina published a fourth short story entitled "Mi escuela" ("My School").[6] in this very brief composition she concentrates on capturing the kind of moment that delights every good teacher: the moment when it becomes obvious to everyone that the entire class has fortuitously but undeniably learned something. This happens almost by definition during those times when the regular curriculum has been suspended and some real communication is allowed to take place. Thus it is that during a particularly suffocating grammar class, Alfonsina decides to warn her students not to chew on the one pencil that they all had to share. She goes on to explain what germs are, and how they are transmitted from one person to another. Looking around at the poverty-stricken children in her class, she warns them that tuberculosis is an especially dangerous disease that seems to flourish in the poor neighborhoods of the city. When she has finished her explanation, a thin, pale boy rises to his feet and says "That is how my mother died." The class is silent as they contemplate the boy's suffering, realizing, perhaps for the first time, that it is possible to control what they had formerly assumed to be the unavoidable tragedies of life. But Alfonsina, seeing things from a different perspective, is one step ahead of them, for she knows that a knowledge of medicine is not sufficient to rescue these underprivileged children from their squalid destinies. As she looks at them, she feels the urge to throw open the windows so that they may escape like butterflies into the blinding sun. Then she realizes that as they sit there in the dark, rectangular classroom, they are all prisoners, bound by three words whose meaning she will never understand as long as she lives: order, system, and discipline.

The year 1919 marked the beginning of a very prolific period in

Alfonsina's life. She published six stories and two short novels, as well as a large number of essays on numerous topics. This was also the year in which she published *Irremediablemente*, the second book of her poetic trilogy. When this volume was discussed in Chapter 2, it was pointed out that many of the poems in the collection dealt with the author's recognition of the fact that her dreams of love could not stand being transplanted to reality for very long, and so her passionate desires would sooner or later turn "irremediably" to ashes. This realization caused her to undergo a feeling of disillusionment bordering on despair, and she resolved several times to renounce altogether the pursuit of what seemed to be a hopeless chimera.

Judging from the content of both her poetry and her prose, 1919 was a year of crisis for Alfonsina, as she struggled with her new insights and with her need to tame the elusive god of love. The short story that best illustrates her frame of mind is given the appropriate title of "Una crisis,"[7] an intriguing composition representing what might be understood as the confrontation of her ego and alter ego. The protagonist, Julia, is a woman who has all the attributes admired by other women in her circle: she is well-born, elegant, vivacious, witty, and talented. She also enjoys an apparently sound marriage to a man who has all the right qualities to ensure their worldly success. Her glamorous life and personality make her very attractive to the opposite sex whose advances she halts with a pleasant, albeit self-satisfied smile. Her self-satisfaction evaporates, however, when she meets her husband's good friend X, for he seems impervious to her many charms. His disinterest kindles her desire, his continued aloofness angers her, and she spends the following year waging a subtle campaign to seduce him in order to get her revenge. She dreams of seeing him lose his composure, of making him break down—and to her utter astonishment her dream eventually comes true. The day after she makes love with him she urgently summons her best friend, María, and confesses everything to her with expressions of the greatest remorse and self-loathing. María consoles her and gives her some sound advice. A few days later the two women meet at a party, and María observes with increasing interest her friend's jovial conversation, which suggests that nothing at all has happened to disturb her usual equanimity. As soon as they are alone together, Julia explains to her that, thanks to her affair with X, she is now firm in her resolve to be faithful to her husband.

Compared to X, with whom she has become completely disillusioned, her husband has acquired a nobility she had not recognized before, and she is now more deeply in love with him than ever.

It would appear that Alfonsina was experimenting here with the idea of channeling the familiar disappointment of satisfied desire into something constructive, thus triumphing over the "irremediable" disenchantment that she described throughout the second volume of the trilogy. Julia believes that her own disillusionment with X has freed her from ever again becoming the victim of the Eros game: "But this [her affair] has liberated me, to my happiness, from all the mistakes that I might have made later on . . . Oh, how I shall love my husband!"[8] Anything is possible, of course, but the reader remains unconvinced by Julia's self-assured declaration. She is by no means as free as she thinks she is, a fact that has not escaped the notice of the author herself, who mentions that Julia has selected her most diaphanous gown to wear to the party that night. She is obviously prepared to become love's victim once again, as soon as an appropriately disinterested Y or Z presents himself. It will then be, perhaps, only a matter of time before she sees through her self-deception and perceives, along with the author, the futility of all game-playing.

A detail in this story might well have passed unnoticed were it not for the fact that Alfonsina underlined it so often in her prose fiction of 1919 that it grew into a regular theme: the infidelity of a partner in an apparently *happy* relationship. This motif is not strongly delineated in "Una crisis" because Julia's sincerity is so obviously in question that the reader does not take seriously the so-called happiness of her marriage, and yet the situation described here by the author foreshadows her growing concern about passion's ability to devastate even the most stable partnerships. Alfonsina illustrates her concern in another short story in letter form, entitled "Carta de una engañada" ("Letter From a Deceived Wife").[9] This is the only story in which the situation is described entirely from the wife's point of view, so it is not really possible to measure the husband's involvement with either his wife or his mistress. But one certainly suspects, judging from what the wife writes in her letter, that he must have felt more than a little dominated by this woman who admits candidly that her outrage arises mainly from the realization that she no longer "owns" her husband. Her jealousy, she says, is not the usual, vulgar jealousy that wives feel in these situations, but one that stems from the loss of the spiritual being she thought she had created, and yet had failed to mold successfully. Once again the happiness of the partnership is only apparent, for even though the wife comforts her remorseful husband and promises to help him forget the other woman, it is clear that his remorse is only a disguise for the despair he feels at having been jilted, while at the same time the wife's forgiveness allows her to wait for an appropriate moment to get revenge on her unsuspecting spouse. The couples in these two stories have a fairly clear record of deceiving both themselves and their mates, so the infidelities do not come as a great surprise.

In strong contrast to these stories, however, are the two short novels that Alfonsina wrote during the year 1919, for in them she is very careful to point out that the lovers have every reason to believe themselves to be happily bound to each other, and yet passion, in spite of everything, manages to get the better of them. In *Un alma elegante (An Elegant Soul)*,[10] she describes the almost utopian marriage enjoyed by Elena, a sensitive, fragile young woman, and Ernesto, who caters to her with old-fashioned gallantry. Suddenly the pleasant harmony of their life together is interrupted by the visit of Elena's cousin Nidia, an athletic, self-confident, rather brash woman who is supposed to be recuperating from the loss of her fiancé. Their peaceful country estate in Cordova is filled with the noise of their guest's daily activities, which she pursues with unending vigor. She constantly tries to squeeze as much excitement as she can from every moment: if she goes riding, she must gallop her horse into a foaming sweat; if she goes for a walk, she must climb up the most dangerous rocks; even if she is swinging on the hammock, she must be pushed until she is almost upside down. Ernesto, fearing the creeping lethargy of middle age, is intrigued by this energetic young creature, but at the same time he is annoyed by the jolting interruptions in his routine. Nidia, meanwhile, is eyeing him with something more than detached interest. "Laughing at the unhappiness of others," explains the author, "she often had the desire to submit herself to a test of her own female power by stealing lovers . . . but nothing inspired in her greater disgust than the spectacle of a conquered man."[11]

At first she contents herself with merely flirting with Ernesto, but although he is flattered and finds her tempting, he is obviously a man of sound common sense and he has no difficulty keeping the situation under control. This, of course, only serves to inspire her to try harder in her self-testing exercise. Then one day when the three of them are out for a walk, Nidia sees an unusual wild flower growing a couple of feet under the edge of a steep cliff. She coquettishly asks Ernesto to get it for her, but Elena intervenes, begging him not to risk his life for such a foolish reason. Not wishing to upset his wife, he quickly accedes to her wishes. With a snort of disdain, Nidia perches herself on the brim of the precipice and plucks the flower, then waves it in front of Ernesto's face with triumphant glee. He experiences a surge of negative emotion, and from that moment on he feels constrained to prove his manliness to the scoffing Nidia. She immediately realizes that she has at last succeeded in getting him involved with her, and the game begins in earnest as each tries to impress the other.

Ernesto, however, is disturbed by his betrayal of Elena, so he is more solicitous than ever in his treatment of her. Fearing, too, that she might sense what is on his mind, and wishing to remind himself of the love he had until so recently freely expressed to her, he makes an eloquent speech to both women about how his wife rescued him from the many illusions he had once harbored as a young man. He had never really known true love, he explains, until Elena taught him what it was all about. Nidia contemplates them both with renewed scorn, then bursts out laughing. She is obviously hurt by his comments about true love, and she looks forward to getting her revenge by proving to him that his speech was a sham from beginning to end. The next day she tells Elena, who is feeling "indisposed," that she plans to steal her husband away and take him for a ride on horseback. Elena understands the irony of this apparently innocent plan much better than Nidia realizes, but she is too proud to show any jealousy of such unworthy competition as her cousin. While they are alone together the next day, Ernesto is puzzled by Nidia's ill humor and reticence to communicate with him, but he optimistically assumes that her interest in him is now so great that she is unable to act naturally in his presence. When they are ready to go home he cannot resist holding her hand a little longer than necessary as he helps her mount, whereupon she violently snatches her hand away from his and gallops back to the stable. To his horror, she mentions the incident to his wife at the dinner table, but Elena pretends to attach no importance to it. Now the game has switched into high gear, for it is no longer a question of impressing each other, but of hurting and getting revenge. What started out to be a mild, controllable sexual desire on Ernesto's part has now turned into an obsessive wish to rape this disdainful little upstart into submission, and one night he manages to make his wish come true. Elena catches him in the act, and Nidia, triumphant, simply packs her bags and goes home, leaving Ernesto and his wife to pick up the pieces.

Many readers might be disappointed that the novel does not end here, but the author continues for many pages to describe Ernesto's infinite remorse and Elena's angelic forgiveness. She is too delicate to survive the emotional shock she has endured, however, so she contracts a fever and finally dies of meningitis. This melodramatic ending dates the composition as a period piece and makes it rather difficult for the modern reader to appreciate it fully. But if one takes into consideration the entire body of Alfonsina's writings in 1919, it is reasonable to conclude that the final pages were not composed merely to appeal to the sentimental readers who expected to shed some tears before closing their books. Instead, she continues the story in order to make a statement about the power that passion can have over even the most happily married people, especially those who, being forewarned by years of experience, consider themselves to be comfortably forearmed and out of danger. It is Ernesto's self-confident belief in his invulnerability to passion, in fact, that triggers Nidia's desire to goad him into seducing her. But not until after the fact did Ernesto do any soul-searching. During the last pages of the book, when Nidia has left their house, he and Elena talk with each other about what had been taking place beneath the surface, and he is amazed to discover how much she had known all the time. He is also miserable when he realizes how deeply he has made her suffer, and for what senseless reasons. "How absurd it all was," he thinks to himself. "If only I had put a stop to it right from the start! Three stupid months, speculating about each other, putting our personal pride into the balance . . . how illogical it all was, how incomprehensible!"[12] This is Ernesto's moment of self-recognition, and the picture that develops fills him with disgust as he realizes, too late of course, that passion is a blinding ego-game over which the players have little control. As for Elena, she cannot resist twisting the knife as she welcomes her impending death as a way to escape from a world which is too vulgar and bestial for her sensitive spirit. She has come to believe that not only does sexual passion present a mere illusion of love, but that love itself is also a cruel and demeaning piece of trickery. Only in fairy tales can two beings "love each other no matter what, with a great, absolute, unique, grandiose love."[13]

This comment is echoed throughout the author's poetic trilogy as well, which serves to underscore the extent to which she was obsessed, in those years, by an all-pervasive, tormented disillusionment with love. The falsity of love, even when it appears to be "great, absolute, unique, and grandiose" is symbolized by the eventual infidelity of one of the partners. Infidelity is the prime enemy, not because it is morally wrong, but because it forces the once-blissful lovers to see each other as they really are: two essentially narcissistic, self-absorbed people, struggling to convince themselves that they alone among mortals have the depth of spirit to experience a love that endures to the end. In the case of Ernesto and Elena, one can appreciate in retrospect that his solicitous courtesy toward his wife is a form of pride, almost as though he were taking satisfaction in his own ability to treat her with the delicacy that only a sensitive person like himself could possibly understand. That same pride is also at the root of his desire to rape Nidia, for he could not abide the thought of being mocked by this young creature who had so insolently challenged his masculinity. As for Elena, she is by no means as free of pride as one might at first assume. Although she knew all along what was on Ernesto's mind, she nevertheless took a masochistic pleasure in saying nothing. "She could have said to her husband, 'come to your senses, she is making fun of you, she scorns you,' and she could have told her cousin that she was a wicked woman. But instead, she contemplated their maneuvers with a sort of morbid paralysis of the will."[14] Rather than warn her husband, for his sake and for her own, that he is playing a dangerous game, she prefers to sit back and watch him get more and more deeply entangled. It is largely pride, and not only curiosity, that makes her want to see how far he will go, for the more she allows him to hurt her, the more she will have the upper hand when the game is over. This, in fact, is exactly how it turns out in the end, for she plays the death-bed scene like a professional. The reader immediately loses all sympathy for her as she ingenuously expresses her infinite self-pity, while she slowly expires before the eyes of her mortified husband. She has achieved a victory, of sorts, for she has managed to reduce Ernesto to a state of utter misery, but she pays for this pitiful triumph with her life. One is reminded here of Nidia's callous plan to seduce him for the express pleasure of seeing him lose his composure, but she also pays for her victory, for as she flounces out of the house it is quite clear that she is embarking on a self-deadening process whose end is not at all in sight. The two women both manage to put Ernesto where they want him, but ironically they, as well as Ernesto, are the victims of their own narcissism.

The infidelity of one of the partners in an apparently happy relationship is the theme once again of the only other short novel Alfonsina was ever to write: *Una golondrina (A Swallow).*[15] The protagonist, Lucila, is another delicate young girl who is over-protected throughout her childhood by her doting parents. When they die, she is totally unprepared to take care of herself or to overcome the despondency that is partly brought on by her own helpless idleness. She accepts the first marriage proposal that comes her way, and her wedding night is the classical one in which the silently weeping bride stares at her husband's broad and impersonal back as he snores contentedly by her side. Things get predictably worse. When he takes to drinking, carousing, and threatening her, the gentle Lucila can stand no more. One day she simply takes her small son by the hand and leaves, and to her immense relief her husband does nothing to locate her afterwards. She finds a job as a receptionist in a law firm where eventually the junior partner falls in love with her. He would have married her, we are told, if she had been free to do so, but since this is not the case, they set up housekeeping together in a lovely chalet, and "with the kind of rare sensitivity in men that women never forget, he consecrated her the companion of his soul."[16] Their life in the chalet is nothing less than idyllic. Lucila is at last able to dedicate herself to caring for her son, and they spend their days reading, talking, practicing the piano, or preparing special dinners for Julián when he comes home in the evening.

But happiness begins to pall, and as Lucila's inner life develops and grows, she feels a restlessness that she cannot explain: "What was that, down in the very depths of her soul, in the dark spiritual well that her thoughts had never dared to explore? Did she have any idea? Had she ever asked herself about it, or put it to a test? The truth is that up until then Lucila had lived without controlling her destiny. But what was this destiny of hers? . . . Perhaps Lucila had not yet asked herself these questions because after suffering so much with her husband, her present life seemed absolutely glorious to her. Once, however, when she was reading a short novel by Francis James called *The Story of a Passionate Young Woman,* she had felt disturbed, preoccupied. That noble and aristocratic young woman, robust and healthy, who throws herself into the arms of a shepherd 'without reservations and without remorse,' had made a deep impression on her . . .'I would like to feel such passion,' she thought."[17] Once this desire finds its way into her conscious mind, it is not long before she meets an appropriately handsome man with intense, penetrating eyes and a melancholy smile, onto whom she hastens to project her romantic fantasies. This young man, Ernesto, happens to be one of Julián's closest and most trusted friends, who is passing through Buenos Aires on his way home to Montevideo. The very impossibility of the situation serves to excite the interest of both Lucila and Ernesto, and their mutual desire grows in proportion to their struggle to deny it. As each begins to realize the strength of the other's passion, they come to foresee, with fear and yearning, that they are doomed some day to yield to each other, in spite of their wish not to betray the love and friendship of Julián. "At times, she felt like confessing everything to her husband. It seemed to her that if she could talk to him about her feelings, and analyze them, and comment freely on them, she could shatter them to pieces, as light is refracted when it passes through cut crystal."[18]

One night, while the three of them are having dinner, Julián is suddenly called away on some urgent business. When Lucila and Ernesto find themselves unexpectedly alone with each other, they are so overcome with emotion that they can barely speak. Their very silence is an obvious declaration of desire, a desire which becomes intolerable when they retire to the living room sofa for their usual after-dinner coffee. If they had planned to meet alone, they might have had time to fortify themselves beforehand against any temptations that might have arisen. But this unexpected opportunity catches them off their guard, and there is no turning back. Their moment has finally come, and they make love to each other. During the days that follow, they are stunned to discover that their passion has grown so strong that it has become a constant obsession. Lucila cannot bear to be separated from her lover at night. She imagines that all the houses between her chalet and his hotel suddenly collapse, leaving a jagged, black wound through the twinkling city lights. Then, within a split second, she and Ernesto would go flashing along the pathway like two magnetized shooting stars, colliding in the middle and lighting up the city with the brilliance of their passion. Ernesto, more sober than his mistress but no less exalted, decides that he must leave for Montevideo without delay. He invites her to see him off; she demurs, but finally goes, against her will and in spite of her better judgment, to the appointed place. The next thing we know she is on the boat to Montevideo with Ernesto, half fainting in his arms. "Oh my friends, forgive her, for in this immense and ever moving life, all is attraction, sympathy, love, change, impulse, madness. . . . It seemed to her that she was born to live this moment, that her life had been created especially so that she could experience this, in spite of everything, against all reason, beyond human judgment. And Time, who knows all the answers and is the complete master of all passions, allowed her to think, dream, laugh, and believe, with the ironic smugness of an old expert."[19]

A year passes, and the chapter opens in Buenos Aires. Julián is watching Lucila's little son playing one of her musical compositions on the piano. In his hand is a dog-eared letter which he has read many times and which Alfonsina now shares with the reader. In it Lucila asks Julián for his forgiveness, implores him to be a father to her son, and tells him that the only thing she can do to be worthy of him is to take her own life. Julián sees a flock of migrating swallows in a mysterious V-formation against the sky. As he contemplates them flying free, bound for some unknown destination, compelled by natural forces to seek a new resting place and a new home, he thinks of his dead mistress.

In this story, as in many others, the modern reader will find that Alfonsina had a tendency to exaggerate the sentimental passages to an embarrassing degree. No matter how distasteful this may be, however, it should be kept in mind that her writing was largely autobiographical, based almost entirely on her own experience and observations, so it was inevitable that her characters should be a direct expression of the highly charged emotions she was feeling during that period of her life. *Una golondrina* is autobiographical even in its details: Lucila is exactly the same age as the author at the time of writing, the fictional son and the real son are also the same age, both Lucila and Alfonsina work for a living, and each has an impediment, real or imagined, to her getting married. But the most noteworthy appearance of Alfonsina herself in her own story has nothing to do with what she had already suffered in her life. Instead, it is an extraordinarily prophetic picture of the circumstances of her own death. "I am going to make myself worthy of both you and him," says the letter, referring to Julián and her son. "I am going to give you the only thing I have, my life. Oh, if only you were here, there might still be time . . . but a horrible wind is blowing, it is cold, the doors and the windows are creaking and the sea has gone mad."[20] Nineteen years later, in Mar del Plata, a cold wind rattled the doors and windows of the house where Alfonsina was staying, and the sea dashed its angry waves onto the pier from which she threw herself. The imaginary demon that made Lucila capable of acting on her wildest impulse by turning her back on her son and her happy life in the chalet, was the same demon that prompted both women, Alfonsina and her literary counterpart, to give up their lives to a sea as frenzied and as turbulent as their own hearts. "Do you find it strange, my friends, that on a stormy night at sea the furious elements should throw the dying swallows onto the decks of passing ships, or that the sea should accept them once and for all into her magnificent bosom? What do you know, what do I know, what do any of us know about swallows, the night, and the sea?"[21]

The image of the swallow was one that appealed greatly to Alfonsina, for it appeared time and again throughout her poetry, especially in the early volumes. The best definition of what the swallow represented for her is found in her first book of poetry, *La inquietud del rosal*, in a poem called simply "Golondrinas" ("Swallows").

They are sweet messengers of sorrow . . .they are black little birds, black as the night, black as pain itself. Sweet swallows who in the winter fly far away across the sea, leaving their nests alone and abandoned!

Las dulces mensajeras de la tristeza son . . .
Son avecillas negras, negras como la noche,
Negras como el dolor.

Las dulces golondrinas que en invierno se van
y que dejan el nido abandonado y solo
Para cruzar el mar!

Obra poética completa, pp. 25–26

Alfonsina indentified with these birds, compelled as they were by some strange and relentless power of nature to abandon the nest and fly away over the sea, restlessly looking for a new life, a new love. Alfonsina herself was forever moving, both emotionally and in the most literal sense, trying to find a feeling of renewal by changing her surroundings at every opportunity.[22] During her younger years she was often beset with the panicky thought that life was somehow passing her by, a fear that she tried to minimize by grimly expanding the perimeters of her endless search. She explored every avenue that promised to lead her to something exciting, or adventurous, or perhaps even tragically overpowering. She tended to see herself as forever soaring high above the stifling mediocrity of the world, and like the swallow she so admired, she could not tolerate the idea of being imprisoned in a cage. The image of the caged bird is one that is easily associated with Alfonsina's writing, due partly to the fact that one of her poems, "Hombre pequeñito" ("Little Man"),[23] has appeared in a large number of anthologies of Latin American poetry. Here the author describes how she feels trapped by her lover's own spiritual and emotional limitations, and she demands that he let her out of the cage at once. "I loved you for half an hour—ask me for nothing more."

There was another kind of cage, however, that disturbed her a good deal more than the one that was so often fashioned by lovers who proved to be unworthy of her. This cage is so universally feared and desired that it has been described variously as "the tender trap," "the tie that binds," and the like. Nevertheless, it is one that should not be overlooked in Alfonsina's case, for it sheds further light on her preoccupation with the failure of the apparently happy relationship. Her search for the *grande passion*, with all its fireworks and combustibility, was complemented by a yearning for a stable, long-lasting love, and yet she was deeply suspicious of becoming hopelessly enmeshed in her own happiness. Stability, she felt, could lead all too easily to stagnation, and nothing seemed to trouble her more than the idea of settling into a safe, predictable pattern. It was the very security of her life in the chalet that prompted Lucila, the protagonist of *Una golondrina*, to ask herself whether there might not be something more waiting for her somewhere else. And yet even after she fell in love with Ernesto, she struggled hard to remain in her gilded cage, for she felt understandably bound by Julián's generosity and her own gratitude for all he had given her. She was drawn more or less equally in both directions, and the tension was finally more than she could bear.

Another story written in 1919, "Carta de una novia" ("Letter From a Bride-To-Be"),[24] focuses on the anxiety of a young girl who is about to be wed, and who foresees that she, too, might find herself trapped by all the conventions of a middle-class marriage. Her premonition hits her with full force two days before her wedding when she goes to inspect the chalet that her fiancé has rented for them. The garden is overgrown, and the house itself is freezing cold, with pieces of furniture scattered here and there, covered with sheets. Her footsteps on the uncarpeted floors echo ominously, and the rain runs drearily down the bare window panes. She feels strangely depressed by those empty, unfamiliar rooms which seem to reflect the hollowness of her future life, and she runs out of the house in tears. Her mother is quick to recognize the source of her apprehension. "We women," she tells her, "were born to get married. My mother did, and so did I, and now you are going to do it too. All the women in our family have always been virtuous, obedient, strong, serene, and silent. Our consciences were so clear that the walls of our houses could have been made of glass. You are like the other women in the family. The moment has come for you to serve God and His law."[25] The bride-to-be bites her lips so as not to scream in frustration at the words of her mother, who is lovingly guiding her to the gates of her future prison. Her wedding gown arrives, there is no going back, everything is settled, it is too late to change her destiny; she is not now, and never has been, in control of her life. Who is this man she is about to marry? She cannot answer her own question because she realizes, too late, that she has been hypocritical throughout her engagement, perhaps even throughout her entire life. "When he comes to call, in spite of my wish to be frank, in spite of my moral values, I take care to make myself more attractive, I weigh what I say, and I try to cover my defects with both word and dress . . . oh, everything is so absurd in this comedy of the sexes!"[26] She will have to pay for a lifetime of game-playing by living in the fetters that she and her family have unknowingly forged, but she finds consolation in the hope that her husband will turn out to be the kind of man who will understand her well enough to be a partner, and not a stranger.

Several months later Alfonsina wrote a sequel to these comments, which she entitled "Carta a una pequeña amiga" ("Letter to a Young Friend").[27] Here she plays the role of the older woman giving advice to a younger friend, and once again she stresses the importance of exercising strict personal honesty in all things, if one is to survive the built-in hypocrisies of society, the family, and most human relationships. If we live by the rules that we are taught, she explains, we end up deceiving ourselves and each other, and then we are condemned to a conventional, meaningless life. Honesty, and the courage to act on it, are the only defenses a thoughtful individual has against the corrosive influences of "inferior minds."

Just how corrosive these influences can be is a matter that Alfonsina examined in some detail a decade later, in a witty story entitled "Psicología de dos centavos" ("Two Cents' Worth of Psychology").[28] She was almost forty years old when she wrote this composition, so by that time her view of passionate love had changed considerably. She was no longer perplexed and disillusioned by its inevitably ephemeral nature. The tone of anger and despair that was evident in her early writing was replaced by a humorous cynicism. She had come to terms with Eros at last, expecting nothing more from him than what he was able to deliver: a moment of excitement, perhaps even one of exaltation, and then, if all went well, a pleasant memory. "Three men," she explains, "are just the right number for a normal, decent woman. Every woman should have at least one premarital affair, then a husband, then another one after her divorce."[29] The narrator of the story, however, has not taken her own advice, and she regrets the many opportunities she lost before she married. She also laments the wasted years during which she spent all her time trying to be a model wife, for she succeeded only in boring her lord and master half to death. It is in the middle of one of his accustomed yawns that she decides to leave him, and in no time at all her bags are packed and she is heading for the country to recuperate. A friend had recommended a rooming house run by a religious old widow and her studious, introverted son. The narrator looks forward to a long rest, during which she expects to be free of even the slightest sexual temptation, for "our greatest accomplishment here on earth is to control perfectly our own passions." So saying, she is overcome with desire for the widow's son, who turns out to be the most beautiful specimen of a human male that she has ever seen. Her imagination runs wild, her thyroid glands leap in her throat, and her heart beats totally out of control. To her infinite delight she begins to realize that the student shares her desire, and her fever rises to 150 degrees (centigrade). At this point the widow develops a headache, and the narrator offers her an analgesic. She looks at the pill very suspiciously, then refuses to take it because she believes it must surely be a sedative. She as much as accuses the narrator of intending to put her to sleep so that she can then get her hands on her son. The narrator feels understandably demeaned by the old woman's insinuations, and the rest of the story is a detailed, tongue-in-cheek analysis of how the widow manages to snuff out the younger woman's desire with her constant barrage of evil-minded accusations.

Judging from Alfonsina's other opinions, both spoken and written, on the subject of the social mores of postwar Argentina, it is not difficult to determine that the widow represented for her all the thoughtless, narrow conventions that she so greatly despised. Passion, as she finally came to understand it, was not only a potentially destructive force, but one which could also serve as a source of great joy and inspiration. Like the fire that so often symbolized it, passionate love could either warm or burn those who yielded to it. Conventional people, however, were thoroughly incapable of seeing the poetic or spiritual components of amorous passion, so lovers were quickly classified by the town gossips as being either rogues or whores, depending on their sex. Alfonsina herself felt that society had placed her altogether too often into the last category, and her annoyance is beautifully reflected in the acrid portrait she draws of the self-righteous widow, determined at any cost to protect her son from the designing woman who is evidently out to get him. The narrator's desire is killed by the false light in which she is seen by the widow, who judges everything according to set formulas. Passion, no matter how universal the rules which govern it, is always as unique as the individuals who succumb to it, and it is absolutely essential that the lovers themselves believe in the uniqueness of their own experience. Once this belief is suspended, then passion is doomed. This is just what happens in the case of the narrator and the student, for the widow interprets their mutual desire as being nothing more than a routine attempt on the part of her guest to make a sexual conquest, and her view of the lovers slowly infects the way they see themselves.

There is another story, entitled simply "Una carta" ("A Letter"),[30] written ten years earlier, in which Alfonsina dissects a love affair that fails for similar reasons. Here the young woman's desire is killed not by the intervention of a third party, but by the lover himself. In a moment of thoughtless candor, he admits using the same technique in wooing a former mistress as the one which in fact had greatly charmed his present partner. Her belief in the uniqueness of their relationship is not only suspended, but altogether shat-

tered, and she is astonished to discover how quickly her desire for
him turns to repugnance. One is reminded once again of Alfonsina's
constant concern about the death of passion which "irremediably"
occurs as a result of boredom, fulfillment, security, routine, and, as
illustrated in the last two stories, disillusionment.

These pitfalls all exist in the real world, of course, so they can only
threaten real relationships. Alfonsina sometimes sought safety from
these dangers in the realm of her own imagination where she could
protect her desire from such assaults. One of the short stories written in 1920, entitled "Tu nombre" ("Your Name"),[31] represents
such a refuge. It is a lengthy poem in prose, a forerunner of the
volume she was to publish in 1926, called *Poemas de amor (Love
Poems)*. In it she describes an early morning walk in the woods,
where, melancholy and lonely, she thinks of the man she loves. At
that very moment he is sleeping peacefully in the arms of another
woman, and she calls his name, hoping somehow to penetrate his
very spirit with her need for him, but the sound of his name is
absorbed by the deep silence of the unmoved and unmovable trees.

One has the feeling, after reading so many compositions about her
disillusionment with passion, that she finds a certain consolation in
her solitude, for here, at least, her desire is safe from the danger of
being killed by happy satisfaction. Judging from the whole picture
that she presents in all her writings on the subject of passionate
love, it would seem she was not so much a woman who ideally
needed three consecutive men in her life, as she declared in
"Psicología de dos centavos." Rather, she gives the impression of
being a woman who would be content to love two men both at once,
if one of them could give her security, understanding, and con-
tinuity, while the other provided all the tantalizing qualities needed
to keep passion at a high pitch: their relationship would have to be
kept secret; there would have to be obstacles, but not unsurmount-
able ones, to their union; and, above all, their love would have to be
taboo. What she appears to need is both a husband and a lover at the
same time, but her writings constantly reveal a scrupulousness and a
sense of fair play that would never permit her to take advantage of
men to satisfy her personal needs. She saw sexual infidelity as a
betrayal of the integrity and the trust of the partner, and she respected men far too much ever to harm them in this way. On the
other hand, she was the kind of woman who could simply not get
along without passionate love. In her own life she chose not to

marry. The evidence suggests that her decision was based on the fact that she was aware, consciously or subconsciously, that she needed the freedom to pursue her passions without victimizing another man. If this was indeed the case, or if it was even partly so, then her denial of marriage must be seen as a sacrifice, for her writing shows that one side of her was always strongly attracted to the many pleasures of the home. If she had married, of course, this also would have represented a sacrifice for her, but it was one that she was not prepared to make.

Her feelings on this matter are clearly stated in one of the letters which appear in the collection that includes *Una golondrina*:[32] "If I were a bit more selfish, if I were more concerned about my financial problems, if I were more afraid of the fearful loneliness that I will have to face some day, I would do as so many other women do [and accept your marriage proposal]."[33] "But," she goes on to explain, "I have acquired certain customs and a way of life which my reason abhors but which I desire through sheer habit. No, the home, and its greatest temptation [children] . . . are not for me."[34] She begs her lover to marry a sweet, simple girl who is not always yearning for the impossible. Only in this way can he find happiness, she believes, although she admits that such a person is not likely to understand him very deeply. She is convinced, however, that if he were to marry her (the writer), he would find himself tied down to a woman whose needs he could not, by definition, fulfill. She sets him free for his own sake, certain that one day he will forget her, and hoping that maybe he will come to understand what she has done. Alfonsina knew she could not save herself from the dictates of her many passions, nor did she even wish to do so at that time. But she could, and apparently did, protect others from becoming unknowingly implicated in her personal decision. Sadly, but predictably enough, her disillusionment with passion was not sufficient to inspire her to overcome her addiction to it, for although it never brought her complete satisfaction, it did offer her moments of exaltation which made up for the emptiness and loneliness that were always with her. In spite of her occasional efforts to renounce Eros once and for all (as evidenced in *Languidez*, for example), her heart was not really in it, and, ironically, her failures were not altogether unwelcome to her.

Alfonsina, in many ways, had the soul of a gambler. Apparent everywhere in her writing are her restless search for excitement, her willingness to live dangerously and play the odds, and her compulsive need to risk everything for the ultimate payoff. In her early years, she even had the gambler's optimistic belief that some day she would hit the jackpot and find the ideal man who would never disillusion her. And, like the gambler, she could not understand people who took the safe road. Where was the heroism of a life spent partly in a nice town house and partly in a beauty parlor? Needless to say, she had no patience at all with the hoards of middle-class women who, she felt, had prostituted themselves for the sake of social status and security. One of her most scathing criticisms of such women appears in a story written in 1919, entitled "Diario de una niña inútil" ("Diary of a Useless Young Lady").[35] The narrator receives a decalogue from a friend of hers, which turns out to be a set of instructions on how to land a husband. It includes bits and pieces of worldly advice such as "Do not bear false testimony, except when uttering praise," and "Do not covet thy neighbor's husband until she becomes a widow." The narrator decides to follow the decalogue to the letter, and after a while the miracle occurs: she catches a husband, but in parentheses she admits that she is not sure whether he is a man or a cricket.

Another prose piece, entitled "Historia sintética de un traje tailleur" ("Synthetic Story of a Tailored Suit"),[36] is written in the same vein. This time the narrator is a lady's suit that enjoys the privilege of expressing its sardonic observations about social customs as it passes from one owner to the next. Even though it prides itself on being singularly perspicacious, it has to admit that there are many aspects of human conduct that surpass its understanding. "My owner had one very peculiar habit. Whenever she shook her head back and forth, I observed that the same comments would issue systematically from her lips afterwards."[37]

It was just this kind of somnambulous, robot behavior that Alfonsina could not tolerate in others. One of her longer short stories, "Cuca en seis episodios" ("Cuca in Six Episodes"),[38] describes the narrator's neighbor, a young woman by the name of Cuca, who lives in a typical middle-class apartment in the city. The narrator is fascinated by the seemingly interminable number of meaningless clichés that Cuca is able to utter, in a toneless, expressionless voice. So great is her fascination, in fact, that she decides to befriend her so that she may get to the bottom of her mysterious vacuity. To her amazement, she discovers that Cuca lives surrounded by equally hollow-headed friends, all of whom appear to spend their days in pursuit of the most frivolous possible goals. The narrator is tempted to take her by the ears and shake her to her senses, but she thinks better of it and decides that for the sake of her own sanity she would be well advised to stay away from Cuca altogether, in spite of the fact that she had not managed to find out how it was that this strange woman seemed to act like a puppet on strings. A few months later, her curiosity is finally satisfied. She meets her fortuitously one day in the street, and after conversing for a while, Cuca bids her good-bye and walks straight into the path of a car. The narrator rushes to the scene to see if she can be of some assistance, and to her horror she discovers that Cuca was beheaded in the accident. She stands there transfixed, for from Cuca's mangled neck there comes pouring forth a thick stream of sawdust.

Six pieces of prose fiction in Alfonsina's repertory have not yet been discussed, and these are not so much short stories as sketches of either characters or isolated situations that happened to catch the author's attention. The first of these, "La madre" ("The Mother"),[39] shows an admirable, and perhaps all too rare, sense of humility on the part of the narrator, who comes to see that her mousy, tight-lipped cousin has a greater sensitivity than she herself does to her child's feelings. Another sketch, "El primer huevo" ("The First Egg"),[40] published later the same year (1920), also deals with the touching humility of the comical protagonist who decides to spare the life of her hen, just fattened for the kill, because she has laid her first egg moments before the intended hour of execution. "Una tragedia de reyes" ("A Tragedy of the Three Wise Men"),[41] describes the shock and pain that a mother feels when her son tells her that he knew all along that she, and not the three wise men, was bringing him presents every year. He continued to deceive her, he explains, because he wanted to make sure that she would go on buying him expensive gifts, worthy of the Magi. The mother is horrified to realize that her son has been imitating her deceptions, but substituting selfish motivations for her own idealistic ones. Alfonsina gives herself away in "Una naranja" ("An Orange"),[42] in which the narrator takes credit for tactfully teaching a country boy how to peel an orange so that he will not embarrass himself when he dines with his betters. Considering the many caustic comments she made about society and its nonsensical regulations, one might have expected her to advise the boy just to be himself and not worry about what people might say. Instead, she reveals a certain hidden snobbery when she deals with the whole question of how an orange should be peeled correctly, which she appears to take as seriously as does her eager young friend. "Don Paulo"[43] is a splendid character study of a cruel and truculent man who viciously beats his son for killing a neighbor's rooster. This he does in front of the neighbor, not because he is interested in punishing the boy, but for the express purpose of getting even with the neighbor for daring to complain about the dead bird.

"Catalina,"[44] the sixth and last of the group of short stories under discussion, may very well be Alfonsina's masterpiece in the genre. In it she describes her stay at an ancient hotel in a steamy forest, a haven for both vacationers and tarantulas alike. The guests are much more concerned about the ubiquitous spiders than the spiders are about them: "The presence of a tarantula was always announced by a special sort of outburst. Feminine voices gave forth loud shrieks of alarm, soon followed by peals of laughter. When they screamed, the spider was alive; when they laughed, it was dead." The narrator considers herself fortunate to be hostess to one of the creatures who turns up on her bedroom wall, and she decides to name it Catalina. It is a particularly large specimen, almost five inches across, with thick, hairy legs and a sinister mouth, half hidden in beautiful, macabre designs. It seems to be stamped on the wall just above her bed, about four inches beneath the ceiling. She observes it for a long time, but her new pet is totally unaware of her existence. She even sings it a tango to attract its attention, but to her great disappointment it ignores her completely. She eventually concludes that it must have gone to sleep, for it has tucked its left legs under its body, extending the right ones to keep its balance. In spite of her growing affection for the spider, she makes sure that her mosquito netting is well in place before she retires for the night. Just before she turns out her reading lamp she notices that it must have awakened, for all six *(sic)* legs are again in their customary position. Over the next two days Catalina advances about a foot every two hours, with mathematical regularity. Faithful to its original altitude on the wall, it makes a slow and methodical circumnavigation of the room, like a miniature Elcano, until it finds itself above the sink. While the narrator arranges her hair at the sink's mirror, she compares her relationship with Catalina to that of St. Francis with his animals, and she cannot help feeling slightly superior to the male guests who promptly commit insecticide *(sic)* in response to the ladies' screams. Lost in her own self-satisfied thoughts, she is unaware of the fact that Catalina has at last taken notice of her, and has for some time been eyeing her green and brown bed jacket, which it evidently mistakes for a tree. Suddenly, with an agility that is wholly out of character, the tarantula leaps onto the narrator's head. She lets out an ear-piercing shriek, flails wildly at her hair, and within a twinkling poor Catalina is lying dead at her feet. The narrator is overcome with a mixture of relief and remorse, so she decides to write this short story in homage to her dead pet tarantula, and in expiation of the arachnicide that she committed.

It is lamentable that Alfonsina did not continue writing short stories, for "Catalina" is a small chef d'oeuvre of humor, style, and timing. Like many other artists, however, she probably attached no importance to what she was able to accomplish with so little effort, not realizing that her creation came easily to her precisely because it reflected the very core of her talent. Instead, she preferred to spend the following year of her life laboring to produce her most hermetic, "intellectual" poetry, which she published in the collection entitled *El mundo de siete pozos (The World of Seven Wells)*. Soon afterwards she developed cancer, and from that moment on her life and her attitudes were radically different from what they were in the early 1930s, when she wrote "Catalina." At that time she could look back on the unhappiness of her younger years with a certain perspective, so the sentimental self-pity that marred her first attempts at prose fiction was absent from her later stories. In its place were the polished style of "Don Paulo" (whose stylistic forerunner was "El primer huevo," published in 1920), the witty insights into human nature found in "Two Cents' Worth of Psychology," and the light-hearted humor of "Catalina." It is certainly a shame, and more than a little surprising, that her prose fiction has never been collected and republished.[45]

II *Essays*

Alfonsina's nonfictional prose is so extensive that the task of organizing a succinct presentation of it becomes almost impossible. She wrote something on the order of one hundred compositions that can variously be categorized as essays, autobiographical sketches, travel accounts, and short commentaries describing her personal views on a number of topical problems. About one third of these were published in the so-called women's pages of *La Nota,* in the sections entitled "Feminidades" and "Vida femenina." Another third came out in *La Nación,* written under the pseudonym of Tao Lao, in a column called "Bocetos femeninos." The rest appeared in newspapers such as *Crítica* and *El Pueblo,* or in various magazines like *Atlántida, Caras y Caretas, Fray Mocho, Hebe, El Hogar, Mundo Argentino, Nosotros, Nuestra Revista, Vida de Hoy,* and *Vida Nuestra.* These essays and articles covered a wide range of themes, including literary criticism, social commentary, women's liberation, and subjects of general interest such as marriage, divorce, illegitimacy, death, and suicide. Much of this material has already been discussed in previous chapters, since it provided an invaluable source of firsthand information about the author. It would be difficult, therefore, to cover this terrain again without repeating what has already been said, for to analyze her nonfictional prose in systematic order is really to write a biography of Alfonsina Storni. Suffice it to say once again that her essays were a faithful reflection of their creator's personality: they were outspoken, daring, often witty, sometimes moving, and usually always written with the clarity of mind that defined the author all through her life.

CHAPTER 5

Final Appraisal

A FTER a careful reading of the entire corpus of Alfonsina Storni's work—her seven volumes of poetry and miscellaneous poems, her dozens of plays and short stories, and her scores of essays and articles—one is left with the feeling that this prodigious output is a perfect testimony to the incredible courage and stubborn determination she had to possess in order to get around the many obstacles that would have prevented lesser women from ever becoming writers at all. This she accomplished by making many painful sacrifices. She was forced to adopt a defiant attitude toward those who held traditional opinions about women and their so-called role, thus inviting much unneeded and undeserved criticism. She had to accept outrageously low wages for long hours of tedious work, during which time she had to leave her son in the care of others. She fought hard and long before she was taken seriously by the male artists and intellectuals of her day, and even then there were many who had reservations about her literary talent. Often they were correct in their judgments, too, for a number of her early works, both in prose and verse, were marred by expressions of mawkish sentimentality and unembarrassed self-involvement. As she acquired more experience and sophistication, however, her writing showed enough improvement to win her prizes and concomitant recognition, and she was cheered along by many well-wishing friends who encouraged and helped her.

Yet in spite of these accomplishments, her ultimate significance as a writer rests not so much with how she expressed herself, as it does with what she stood for and what she was as a human being. Thousands of women readers saw her as a model of what they or their friends or daughters could hope to achieve some day, and if Alfonsina herself never really became one of the world's greatest writers, it was partly because she spent a good deal of her time and energy opening the way for those who would eventually follow. Other women poets like Delmira Agustini, Juana de Ibarbourou, and Gabriela Mistral were also challenging male hegemony in the fields of art and literature, but it was Alfonsina who actually put her mind to expressing, in clear-headed, no-nonsense prose, the need for feminist action in an unjust society.

It is ironic, but perhaps not surprising, that she should be remembered today only for her poetry, when so much of value is to be found in her plays and prose fiction. It was in these latter genres that she revealed her best insights into social sham and human failure, and it was here that she made her most important contribution to her nation's culture. Since much of what she wrote directly criticized men and the hypocrisy that so often governed their lives, her reviewers tended either to ignore her opinions or to counter-attack what they interpreted as being an assault on their integrity. This reaction on their part was particularly noticeable in the scathing reviews that greeted the opening of her play, *El amo del mundo,* and time did not seem to repair the initial damage suffered by their male egos, even though Alfonsina tried on many occasions to point out that she never hesitated to criticize women, too. Apparently the male critics only took umbrage at what pertained to themselves, and many were quite content to see this excellent body of writing safely relegated to oblivion. She was usually dismissed by such men as being an embittered woman who blamed the members of their sex for her self-imposed unhappiness, but they never read what she wrote carefully enough to realize that she was speaking of the human condition itself, and not that of women alone, when she pointed out the many ways in which we all cause our own and one another's suffering.

Even though Alfonsina had not read widely and probably was not familiar with the major feminist authors in the rest of the world, much of her writing, particularly the nonfictional prose, situates her in the mainstream of feminism. Her concern about women's rights and the servility to which women are condemned by years of conditioning is reminiscent of Mary Wollstonecraft; her views on marriage are similar to those of Lucy Stone; and it would be difficult not to draw comparisons between *El amo del mundo* and Ibsen's *A Doll's House.* Faithful to her own character, Alfonsina almost always treated problems of female emancipation from the point of view of the individual. Ironically, she was sometimes criticized for not placing the whole question of women in a more philosophical perspective, as did John Stuart Mill, for example. Nor did she approach the matter from a political or sociological standpoint, in the tradition of Friedrich Engels, or August Bebel, or Thorstein Veblen. Instead, she preferred to analyze the purely psychological difficulties encountered by both men and women as a result of what must rightly be considered the ridiculous legacy of social custom and training that was handed down from generation to generation. Like many other feminists, she deplored the fact that women were uselessly condemned to a totally unproductive life, their only role being to raise children and to crown their menfolk with laurels that had no meaning, since they were blindly bestowed by ignorant creatures who could not possibly know their true worth. She was convinced that life could be infinitely improved by the institution of some real teamwork between men and women, and that both sexes would stand to gain intellectually, spiritually, and emotionally by dealing with each other as equals. It is a tribute to her depth of insight and the passion with which she expressed herself that so many men and women in Argentina agree with her today.

Notes and References

Chapter One

1. A copy of the original birth certificate, registered by her father on May 31, 1892, was published in *Cronaca Ticinese,* Buenos Aires, November, 1938, and subsequently in *Nosotros* 8 (December 1938): p. 102. In 1938 an aunt had the birth date legally changed to May 22, apparently basing the change on her own memory of the event forty-six years later, and an amended birth certificate was filed. A photograph of the amended document was taken by Edgardo Roncoroni, who published an article about it in *La Nación,* October 20, 1963. The photograph is now in the archives of *La Nación.* Although some biographers now refer to her birth date as being May 22, there seems to be no legal document to back up the aunt's claim that the original birth certificate was in error. Alfonsina herself, according to her son, was of the firm opinion that she was born on May 29.

2. Some of the factual commentary in this section is based on Zulma Núñez, "Así era Alfonsina," which came out in serial form in *Mundo Argentino,* Buenos Aires, starting with year 44, number 2242, February 3, 1954. Part of this was also published in the magazine *Alfonsina* in the October, November, and December issues of 1953. Reference is also made to Conrado Nalé Roxlo and Mabel Mármol, *Genio y figura de Alfonsina Storni* (Buenos Aires, 1964).

3. Alfonsina Storni, "De mi padre se cuenta," ("They Say of My Father") *Ocre,* published in *Obra poética completa* (Buenos Aires, 1961), pp. 264–265. All further quotes and page numbers will refer to this edition.

4. Translations are mine, except where otherwise indicated.

5. Anecdote recounted by Alfonsina Storni in her article, "Entre un par de maletas a medio abrir y la manecilla del reloj," *Revista Nacional,* Montevideo (27 January 1938), pp. 214–215.

6. "Entre un par de maletas . . .", p. 215.

7. Ibid., p. 215.

8. Pedro Alcazar Civit, "Las grandes figuras nacionales: Alfonsina Storni," *El Hogar* (11 September 1931), p. 8.

9. Ibid., p. 8.

10. Quoted by Conrado Nalé Roxlo y Mabel Mármol, *Genio y figura de Alfonsina Storni* (Buenos Aires, 1964), p. 40.

11. Alberto Palcos, *La vida emotiva* Buenos Aires: Gleizer, 1925), p. 190.

12. Pedro Alcazar Civit, p. 8.

13. Quoted by Nalé Roxlo y Mármol, p. 42.

14. Ibid, p. 44.

15. Ibid, p. 46.

16. Alfonsina Storni, *Poemas de amor*, poema II, Buenos Aires, 1926.

17. "The section of consumer psychology," explains Alfonsina, "attempted to determine the requirements of the various consumer markets of the country, in order to adjust accordingly their advertisements, bargains, sales, etc." Pedro Alcazar Civit, p. 8.

18. Alfonsina Storni, *El amo del mundo*, in *Bambalinas*, Buenos Aires, year 9, no. 470 (16 April 1927).

19. Ibid, p. 13.

20. The best-known Anarchist pamphlet was *Humanidad*, published in Buenos Aires. Articles were signed "Una Rebelde" (March 1928), "Enriqueta Marc" (September 1927), and "Irene Boris" (July 1928).

21. *El amo del mundo*, p. 22.

22. Storni, "Sobre el matrimonio," *La Nota*, 5, no. 209, (15 August 1919), p. 854.

23. Tao Lao (pseudonym for Alfonsina Storni), "El varón," *La Nación*, 2nd section (12 June 1921), p. 5.

24. Tao Lao, "La mujer enemiga de la mujer," *La Nación*, 2nd section (22 May 1921), p. 4.

25. The following information about her relationship with her son stems from a series of personal interviews I had with him in Buenos Aires in June, 1975.

26. Eduardo González Lanuza, "Ubicación de Alfonsina Storni," *Sur*, no. 50 (November 1938), pp. 55–56.

27. Pedro Alcazar Civit, "Las grandes figuras nacionales: Alfonsina Storni," *El Hogar* (11 September 1931), p. 8.

28. Storni, "Entretelones de un estreno," *Nosotros*, year 21, 56, no. 215 (April 1927), p. 53.

29. *El Hogar* (24 June 1927).

30. Storni, "Las heroinas," *La Nación*, 2nd section (18 April 1920).

31. Roberto Giusti, "Alfonsina Storni," *Nosotros*, 2nd epoch, year 3, 8, no. 32 (November 1938), pp. 372–373.

32. For a summary of the feminist movement in Latin America, see Lewis Hanke, *History of Latin American Civilization* (Boston: Little, Brown, 1973).

33. Storni, "Votaremos," *La Nota* (12 September 1919).

34. See Eduardo González Lanuza, "Ubicación de Alfonsina Storni," *Sur*, no. 50 (November 1938), pp. 55–56.

35. Enrique Anderson Imbert, *Historia de la literatura hispanoamericana* México-Buenos Aires (Fondo de Cultura Económica, 1954), p. 274.

36. Storni, "Un caso," *La Nota*, 5, no. 216 (3 October 1919), p. 1031.

37. Tao Lao (pseudonym for Alfonsina Storni), "La irreprochable," *La Nación*, 2nd section (5 September 1920), p. 6.

38. Tao Lao, "Las casaderas," *La Nación*, 2nd section (8 August 1920), p. 4.

39. Storni, "Feminismo perfumado," *La Nota*, 4, no. 195 (2 May 1919), p. 530.

40. Storni, "Algunas palabras," *Atlántida*, year 3, no. 116 (14 June 1920).

41. Tao Lao, "Tijereteo," *La Nación*, 2nd section, (19 June 1921), p. 4.

42. Ibid.

43. Storni, "Cositas sueltas," *La Nota*, 4, no. 203 (4 July 1919), p. 713.

44. Ibid.

45. Ibid.

46. María Teresa Orosco, *Alfonsina Storni* (Buenos Aires, 1940), p. 239.

47. "Cositas sueltas," p. 713.

48. "Me siento con ánimos de empezar de nuevo," *El Pueblo*, Montevideo (23 February 1935).

49. "Palabras a Delmira Agustini," *Ocre*, 1925.

50. Quoted by Nalé Roxlo y Mármol, *Genio y figura de Alfonsina Storni* (Buenos Aires, 1964), p. 90.

51. Information based on a personal interview with Alejandro Storni.

52. Storni, *Teatro Infantil* (Buenos Aires, 1950).

53. "Con *El amo del mundo* se presentará mañana en el Cervantes la compañía Fanny Brena," *Ultima Hora* (9 March 1927).

54. Storni, *Cimbelina en 1900 y pico* and *Polixena y la cocinerita*, both published in *Dos farsas pirotécnicas* (Buenos Aires, 1932); *Blanco . . . negro . . . blanco*, published in *Teatro Infantil;* and *La técnica de Mister Dougall*, soon to be published by Ramón Roggero, Sociedad Editora Latino Americana, Buenos Aires.

55. Information based on a personal interview with Blanca de la Vega.

56. See in particular the article from *La Voz*, quoted in *El Diario Español*, (17 January 1930).

57. "De regreso de Europa, Alfonsina Storni nos confía algunas impresiones," *La Nación* (14 March 1930).

58. Ibid.

59. "En el Cap Arcona llegaron Alfonsina Storni . . . y otras personas conocidas," *La Razón* (13 March 1930).

60. "Me siento con ánimos de empezar de nuevo," *El Pueblo*, Montevideo (23 February 1935).

61. Pedro Alcazar Civit, "Las grandes figuras nacionales: Alfonsina Storni," *El Hogar* (11 September 1931).

62. Nalé Roxlo y Mármol, *Genio y figura de Alfonsina Storni* (Buenos Aires, 1964), p. 132.

63. Storni, *Obra poética completa* (Buenos Aires, no date), p. 436.

64. Storni, "Entre un par de maletas a medio abrir y la manecilla del reloj," *Revista Nacional*, Montevideo (27 January 1938).

65. See Zulma Núñez, "Tenía el pudor del sufrimiento," and Carlos Vega, "Parecía empeñada en guardar su secreto," both published in *El Pregón*, Buenos Aires (25 October 1938), p. 7.

66. Copies of these letters were given to me by Alejandro Storni.

67. *Obra poética completa*, p. 440.

68. Information based on a personal interview with Alejandro Storni.

69. Storni, "Alrededor de la muerte de Leopoldo Lugones," *Nosotros*, year 3, 7, no. 26–28 (May–June 1938), p. 220.

Chapter Two

1. Enrique González Martínez, *Los senderos ocultos*, Mexico, 1911.

2. Eduardo González Lanuza, "Ubicación de Alfonsina Storni," *Sur*, no. 50 (November 1938), p. 56.

3. Ibid., p. 55.

4. "Con Alfonsina Storni," interview published in *Myriam*, Buenos Aires (August 1919).

5. Ibid.

6. Storni, "Entre un par de maletas a medio abrir y la manecilla del reloj," *Revista Nacional*, Montevideo (27 January 1938), p. 217.

7. Ernesto de la Fuente, "La poesía y la prosa de Alfonsina Storni," *El Suplemento*, date unknown (from the personal files of Julieta Gómez Paz). Since the writer later speaks of her "latest book" *Ocre*, the interview probably took place shortly after 1925.

8. Nicolás Coronado, "*La inquietud del rosal*, por Alfonsina Storni," *Nosotros*, year 10, 31, no. 83 (March 1916), pp. 406–407.

9. Roberto Giusti, "Alfonsina Storni," *Nosotros*, 2nd epoch, year 3, 8, no. 32 (November 1938), p. 375.

10. León Benarós, "Vida entre dos cartas," *La Nación* (Revista), 6 August 1972.

11. "Entre un par de maletas. . . ", p. 216.

12. Storni, *El dulce daño*, 2nd edition (Buenos Aires, 1920), p. 7.

13. "Queja," *El dulce daño*, p. 108.

14. César Fernández Moreno, "Dos épocas en la poesía de Alfonsina Storni," *Revista Hispánica Moderna*, New York, year 24, no. 1 (January 1958), pp. 27–28.

15. From her letter to R. Brenes Mesén, published in *Revista Iberoamericana*, México, 1, no. 1 (1939), p. 14.

16. Luis María Jordán, "Alfonsina Storni," *Nosotros*, year 13, 32, no. 21 (May 1919), p. 37.

17. Comment made to me during a personal interview in Buenos Aires, in June, 1975.

18. Jordán, p. 40.

19. Roberto Giusti, "Alfonsina Storni," *Nosotros*, 2nd epoch, year 3, 8, no. 32 (November 1938), p. 377.

20. See a pioneering book in the study of passion in literature: Denis de Rougemont, *Love in the Western World*, first published in French in 1940, reprinted in English by Fawcett, New York, 1966. See also the first volume of Otis Green, *Spain and the Western Tradition*, University of Wisconsin Press, 1968.

21. Giusti, p. 378.

22. Baldomero Sanín Cano, "*Ocre*, de Alfonsina Storni," *La Nación*, 3rd section (14 June 1925), p. 5.

23. Ibid.

24. From "Traición," *Ocre*, p. 286.

25. From "Una vez más," *Ocre*, p. 276.

26. Ibid.

27. From "El engaño," *Ocre*, p. 275.

28. Carmen Sidonie Rosenbaum, *Modern Women Poets of Spanish America* (New York, 1945), p. 213.

29. Storni, *Poemas de amor* (Buenos Aires, 1926), poem XLII.

30. For some specific examples of Baudelaire's influence on her poetry, see Helena Percas, *La poesía femenina argentina* (Madrid, 1958), pp. 210–211.

31. Janice Geasler Titiev, *A Critical Approach to the Poetry of Alfonsina Storni*, unpublished doctoral dissertation, University of Michigan, 1972, pp. 118–141.

32. Pedro Alcazar Civit, "Las grandes figuras nacionales: Alfonsina Storni," *El Hogar* (11 September 1931), p. 8.

33. *Poemas de amor*, poema XVIII.

34. Salomon Wapnir, *Crítica positiva*, (Buenos Aires: Editorial Tor, 1926), p. 46, footnote 1.

35. Titiev, *A Critical Approach. . .* , pp. 160–161.

36. Julieta Gómez Paz, "Poemas con danzas," in *Leyendo a Alfonsina Storni* (Buenos Aires, 1966), p. 22.

37. Giusti, "Alfonsina Storni," p. 389.

38. Ibid., p. 391.

39. Ibid., p. 387.

40. Augusto González Castro, "*Mascarilla y trébol*, de Alfonsina Storni," *El Hogar*, Buenos Aires (21 October 1938).

41. *Crítica*, Buenos Aires (25 October 1938).

Chapter Three

1. Octavio Ramírez, "Se presentó en el *Cervantes* la compañía Fanny Brena," *La Nación*, Buenos Aires (11 March 1927).

2. Storni, "Cuca en seis episodios," *La Nación* (11 April 1926).
3. Storni, "Aclaraciones sobre *El amo del mundo,*" *La Nación* (11 April 1926).
4. Storni, *El amo del mundo, Bambalinas,* Bueno Aires, year 9, no. 470 (16 April 1927), p. 22. All subsequent page numbers refer to this publication.
5. Storni, "Entretelones de un estreno," *Nosotros,* year 21, 56, no. 215 (April 1927), p. 53.
6. Ibid., p. 54.
7. From a personal interview with Blanca de la Vega, who taught acting at the Escuela Normal de Lenguas Vivas, and who became a close friend of Alfonsina's.
8. Storni, *Dos farsas pirotécnicas: Cimbelina en 1900 y pico* (Buenos Aires, 1932).
9. Ramón Roggero is presently preparing an edition of Alfonsina's complete works in prose, to be published by the Sociedad Editora Latino Americana, Bs. As. This edition will include *El amo del mundo,* as well as her other plays, essays, articles, short stories, and letters.
10. Her son Alejandro recalls that she was working on *Dougall* while they were living in an apartment which they later vacated toward the end of 1927.
11. It will be included in Ramón Roggero's edition of the complete works in prose, op. cit.
12. See interview entitled "Alfonsina Storni pasa al teatro," *Crítica* (9 April 1931).
13. Ibid.
14. "Alfonsina Storni explica las dificultades de las escritoras para estrenar en nuestros teatros," *La Razón* (7 August 1931).
15. See Eduardo González Lanuza, "Ubicación de Alfonsina Storni," *Sur,* Buenos Aires, no. 50 (November 1938).
16. See Felix Luna, *De Perón a Lanusse* Editorial Planeta (Buenos Aires: 1974).
17. Although the book bears no date of publication, María Teresa Orosco believes it was published in 1931 (*Alfonsina Storni* (Buenos Aires, 1940), p. 282). In her interview with *La Razón* on August 7, 1931 (op. cit.), however, Alfonsina does not mention its imminent publication, so the likelihood is that it came out the following year.
18. Storni, *Dos farsas pirotécnicas,* Cooperativa Editorial Buenos Aires, Cabaut y Cía., 1932. Page numbers cited in the text will refer to this edition.
19. *La Nación* (7 December 1938).
20. *Crítica* (7 December 1938).
21. *La Prensa* (7 December 1938).
22. *La Razón* (7 December 1938).

23. *El Mundo* (7 December 1938).

24. The original manuscripts are in the archives of the Teatro Lavardén in Buenos Aires. María Teresa Orosco (*Alfonsina Storni* [Buenos Aires, 1940], p. 295) notes that her examination of these manuscripts indicates that the plays were composed very quickly.

25. A collection of her children's plays was published under the title *Teatro infantil* by Ramón Roggero y Cía., Buenos Aires, 1950.

26. Arturo Capdevila, *Alfonsina; época, dolor, y obra de la poetisa* (Buenos Aires, 1948), pp. 85–99.

27. Ibid., p. 91.

28. Ibid., p. 91.

29. *Obra poética completa, Irremediablemente* (Buenos Aires, no date), p. 165.

30. Storni, *Teatro infantil*, p. 150.

31. Ibid., p. 161.

32. Ibid., p. 156.

Chapter Four

1. Storni, "De la vida," *Fray Mocho* (10 April 1912).

2. "Una carta," *La Nota*, 2, no. 60 (30 October 1916), pp. 1187–88.

3. "Algunas líneas," *La Nota*, 2, no. 66 (11 November 1916), pp. 1307–1308.

4. "La fina crueldad," *La Nota*, 2, no. 69 (2 December 1916), pp. 1363–1366.

5. See her letter to León Benarós, "Vida entre dos cartas," *La Nación* (Revista), 6. August 1972.

6. "Mi escuela," *Atlántida* (21 November 1918).

7. "Una crisis," *La Nota*, 4, no. 186 (7 March 1919), pp. 221–223.

8. Ibid., p. 223.

9. "Carta de una engañada," *La Nota*, 5, no. 211 (29 August 1919), pp. 899–900.

10. *Un alma elegante, La novela elegante*, no. 3, year 1, Buenos Aires (15 December 1919).

11. Ibid., Chapter Three (no pagination).

12. Ibid., Chapter Ten.

13. Ibid., Chapter Ten.

14. Ibid., Chapter Seven.

15. *Una golondrina, Hebe* (Buenos Aires, no. 7, 1919), pp. 3–26. Republished by the Instituto Amigos del Libro Argentino (*Cinco cartas y Una golondrina* [Buenos Aires, 1959]).

16. *Cinco cartas. . .* , p. 53.

17. Ibid., pp. 56–57.

18. Ibid., p. 63.

19. Ibid., pp. 70–71.

20. Ibid., p. 74.
21. Ibid., p. 75.
22. Her constant moves from one address to another were mentioned by her son, Alejandro Storni, in a personal interview.
23. Storni, *Irremediablemente*, in *Obra poética completa*, p. 165.
24. "Carta de una novia," *La Nota*, 4. no. 197 (16 May 1919), pp. 567–568.
25. Ibid., p. 568.
26. Ibid., p. 568.
27. "Carta a una pequeña amiga," *La Nota*, 5, no. 22 (31 October 1919), pp. 1126–1127.
28. "Psicología de dos centavos," *Crítica* (4 April 1931).
29. Ibid.
30. "Una carta," *La Nación* (24 July 1921).
31. "Tu nombre," *Caras y Caretas*, year 23, no. 1160 (25 December 1920).
32. *Cinco cartas y Una golondrina* (Buenos Aires, 1959).
33. Ibid., p. 10.
34. Ibid., pp. 11–12.
35. "Diario de una niña inútil," *La Nota*, 4, no. 198 (23 May 1919), pp. 596–597.
36. "Historia sintética de un traje tailleur," *La Nota*, 4, no. 199 (30 May 1919), pp. 620–621.
37. Ibid., p. 621.
38. "Cuca en seis episodios," *La Nación* (11 April 1926).
39. "La madre," *La Nación* (11 July 1920).
40. "El primer huevo," *Atlántida* (16 December 1920).
41. "Una tragedia de reyes," *La Nación* (9 January 1921).
42. "Una naranja," *La Nación* (17 July 1921).
43. "Don Paulo," *La Nación* (25 January 1925).
44. "Catalina," *La Nación* (2 April 1933).
45. Ramón Roggero is presently preparing an edition of her complete works in prose, to be published by the Sociedad Editora Latino Americana, Buenos Aires.

Selected Bibliography

PRIMARY SOURCES

For an extensive bibliography, see Marta Baralis, *Contribución a la bibliografía de Alfonsina Storni,* Fondo Nacional de las Artes, Buenos Aires, 1964. For additional titles, particularly the most recent ones, consult the annual bibliography in the *Publications of the Modern Language Association* and *The Year's Work in Romance Languages and Literatures.*

1. Poetry

Obra poética completa. Buenos Aires: Meridión, 1961.
Antología poética (compiled by Alfonsina Storni). Buenos Aires: Espasa-Calpe Argentina, 1938. Buenos Aires: Losada, 1956.
Los mejores versos. Cuadernillos de Poesía no. 21. Buenos Aires: Nuestra América, 1958.
Poesías de Alfonsina Storni. Prologue by Alejandro Alfonso Storni. Buenos Aires: Editorial Universitaria de Buenos Aires, 1961.
La inquietud del rosal. Buenos Aires: La Facultad, 1916.
El dulce daño. Buenos Aires: Sociedad Cooperativa Editorial Limitada, 1918.
Irremediablemente . . . . Buenos Aires: Sociedad Cooperativa Editorial Limitada, 1919.
Languidez. Buenos Aires: Sociedad Cooperativa Editorial Limitada, 1920.
Ocre. Buenos Aires: Babel, 1925.
Poemas de amor (poetry in prose). Buenos Aires: Nosotros, 1926.
Mundo de siete pozos. Buenos Aires: Tor, 1934.
Mascarilla y trébol. Buenos Aires: El Ateneo (printed by Mercatali), 1938.

2. Theater

El amo del mundo. Bambalinas, year 9, no. 470, Buenos Aires (16 April 1927).
La técnica de Mister Dougall (unpublished), 1927.
Dos farsas pirotécnicas. Buenos Aires: Cooperativa Editorial "Buenos Aires," 1932. Contains: *Cimbelina en 1900 y pico* and *Polixena y la cocinerita.*

Teatro infantil. Buenos Aires: Editorial Ramón J. Roggero y Cía., 1950.
Contains: *Blanco . . . negro . . . blanco, Pedro y Pedrito, Jorge y su conciencia, Un sueño en el camino, Los degolladores de estatuas, El dios de los pájaros.*
La sirvienta moderna, La sirvienta mecánica, Los cazadores de fieras. Unpublished children's plays.
Intermedio poético. Produced between the acts of *Judith,* by Carlos Cucullu, which opened at the Teatro Colón on August 18, 1938.

3. Prose Fiction
"De la vida." *Fray Mocho* (10 April 1912).
"Una carta." *La Nota,* 2, no. 60 (30 October 1916).
"Algunas líneas." *La Nota,* 2, no. 66 (11 November 1916).
"La fina crueldad." *La Nota,* 2, no. 69 (2 December 1916).
"Mi escuela." *Atlántida* (21 November 1918).
"Una crisis." *La Nota,* 4, no. 186 (7 March 1919).
"Carta de una engañada." *La Nota,* 5, no. 211 (29 August 1919).
Un alma elegante. In *La novela elegante,* no. 3, year 1, Buenos Aires (15 December 1919).
Cinco cartas y Una golondrina. Buenos Aires: Instituto Amigos del Libro Argentino, 1959. *Una golondrina* was originally published in *Hebe,* no. 7, Buenos Aires, 1919.
"Carta de una novia." *La Nota,* 4, no. 197 (16 May 1919).
"Diario de una niña inútil." *La Nota,* 4, no. 198 (23 May 1919).
"Historia sintética de un traje tailleur." *La Nota,* 4, no. 199 (30 May 1919).
"Carta a una pequeña amiga." *La Nota,* 5, no. 22 (31 October 1919).
"La madre." *La Nación* (11 July 1920).
"El primer huevo." *Atlántida* (16 December 1920).
"Tu nombre." *Caras y Caretas,* year 23, no. 1160 (25 December 1920).
"Una tragedia de reyes." *La Nación* (9 January 1921).
"Una naranja," *La Nación* (17 July 1921).
"Una carta." *La Nación* (24 July 1921).
"Don Paulo." *La Nación* (25 January 1925).
"Cuca en seis episodios." *La Nación* (11 April 1926).
"Psicología de dos centavos." *Crítica* (4 April 1931).
"Catalina." *La Nación* (2 April 1933).

4. Nonfictional prose
Because Alfonsina Storni wrote nearly one hundred nonfictional prose compositions, this section is limited to those essays and articles already mentioned in this book.
"Feminismo perfumado." *La Nota,* 4, no. 195 (2 May 1919).
"Cositas sueltas." *La Nota,* 4, no. 203 (4 July 1919).
"Sobre el matrimonio." *La Nota,* 5, no. 209 (15·August 1919).

"Votaremos." *La Nota*, 5, no. 213 (12 September 1919).
"Un caso." *La Nota*, 5, no. 216 (3 October 1919).
"Las heroinas." *La Nación*, 2nd section (18 April 1920).
"Algunas palabras." *Atlántida*, year 3, no. 116 (14 June 1920).
"Las casaderas." *La Nación*, 2nd section (8 August 1920).
"La irreprochable." *La Nación*, 2nd section (5 September 1920).
"La mujer enemiga de la mujer." *La Nación*, 2nd section (22 May 1921).
"El varón." *La Nación*, 2nd section (12 June 1921).
"Tijereteo." *La Nación*, 2nd section (19 June 1921).
"Entretelones de un estreno." *Nosotros*, year 21, 56, no. 215 (April 1927).
"Entre un par de maletas a medio abrir y la manecilla del reloj." *Revista Nacional*, Montevideo (27 January 1938).
"Alrededor de la muerte de Leopoldo Lugones." *Nosotros*, year 3, 7, no. 26–28, (May–July 1938).

SECONDARY SOURCES

1. Books and monographs

CAPDEVILA, ARTURO. *Alfonsina; época, dolor y obra de la poetisa Alfonsina Storni*. Buenos Aires: Centurión, 1948. Good overall study, with many personal reminiscences. Strong chapters on biography and theater.
GÓMEZ PAZ, JULIETA. *Leyendo a Alfonsina Storni*. Buenos Aires: Losada, 1966. A collection of absolutely first-rate essays on her poetry.
NALÉ ROXLO, CONRADO, and MABEL MARMOL. *Genio y figura de Alfonsina Storni*. Buenos Aires: Editorial Universitaria de Buenos Aires, 1966. A very good biographical study and general critical analysis of her work. Sloppy research.
OROSCO, MARÍA TERESA. *Alfonsina Storni*. Vol. 2, no. 4. Buenos Aires: Instituto de Literatura Argentina (Universidad de Buenos Aires), 1940. A very good general overview of her work, with plot summaries and wide reference to critical opinion. Sketchy bibliography.
PERCAS, HELENA. "Alfonsina Storni." Chapter Two in her *La poesía femenina argentina (1810–1950)*. Madrid: Ediciones Cultura Hispánica, 1958. This book-length chapter (154 pages) is one of the best studies of her poetry. Clear, well-written, carefully researched analysis of life, works, themes, and literary influences.
TITIEV, JANICE GEASLER. *A Critical Approach to the Poetry of Alfonsina Storni*. Unpublished doctoral dissertation, University of Michigan, 1972. An excellent stylistic analysis.

2. Articles

CORONADO, NICOLÁS. "*La inquietud del rosal*, por Alfonsina Storni." *Nosotros*, year 10, 31, no. 83 (March 1916). The first critic to recognize her talent.
———. "*Irremediablemente . . .* por Alfonsina Storni." *Nosotros*, year 13,

32, no. 121 (May 1919). Foresees that she will have difficulty convincing others to overcome their prejudices against intellectual women.

CUENCA, HECTOR. "Alfonsina Storni." *Nosotros*, 2nd epoch year 4, 11, no. 44–45 (November–December 1939), pp. 227–230. Incisive commentary and personal reminiscences.

ESTRELLA GUTIÉRREZ, FERMÍN. "Alfonsina Storni: Su vida y su obra." In his *Estudios literarios*. Buenos Aires: Academia Argentina de Letras, 1969. General survey with personal reminiscences.

FERNÁNDEZ MORENO, CÉSAR. "Dos épocas en la poesía de Alfonsina Storni." *Revista Hispánica Moderna*, 24 (1958), pp. 27–35. Slightly condescending but generally helpful article.

FIGUEIRA, GASTÓN. "La intensa poesía de Alfonsina Storni." *La Nueva Democracia*, New York, year 19, no. 7 (1938), pp. 12–14. Refreshingly original commentary in a year when many repetitive homages were pouring off the presses.

GÁLVEZ, MANUEL. "Alfonsina Storni." *Nosotros*, year 3, no. 32 (November 1938), pp. 369–371. Personal reminiscences and biographical data.

GHIANO, JUAN CARLOS. *Poesía argentina del siglo veinte*, pp. 62–69. Buenos Aires: Fondo de Cultura Económica, 1957. Some perceptive comments.

GIUSTI, ROBERTO. "Alfonsina Storni." *Nosotros*, year 3, no. 32 (November 1938), pp. 372–397. Republished in his *Literatura y vida* (Buenos Aires: Editorial Nosotros, 1939), pp. 97–133. Excellent commentary written by a personal friend and intelligent critic.

GONZÁLEZ LANUZA, EDUARDO. "Ubicación de Alfonsina." *Sur*, Buenos Aires, no. 50 (November 1938), pp. 55–57. First-rate but somewhat unsympathetic.

JORDÁN, LUIS MARÍA. "Alfonsina Storni." *Nosotros*, year 13, 32, no. 21 (May 1919), pp. 37–41. An extremely enthusiastic review. Praises her for not following the fashions of the day.

MAÑACH, JORGE. "Liberación de Alfonsina Storni." *Revista Iberoamericana*, México, 1, no. 1 (May 1939), pp. 73–76. Very good. Talks about the disillusionment of her life.

ROSENBAUM, CARMEN SIDONIE. "Alfonsina Storni." In her *Modern Women Poets of Spanish America*, pp. 205–227. New York: Hispanic Institute, 1945. The first study ever written in English, it also happens to be an excellent discussion of her life, works, and themes.

SCHULTZ DE MANTOVANI, FRYDA. "Alfonsina Storni en el teatro para niños." *La Nación*, 2nd section (19 March 1939). Good commentary on children's theater.

STORNI, ALEJANDRO ALFONSO. Prologue to *Poesías de Alfonsina Storni*. Buenos Aires: Editorial Universitaria de Buenos Aires, 1961. Personal reminiscences written by her son.

VILLARINO, MARÍA DE. Prologue to *Alfonsina Storni; antología.* Buenos Aires: Ediciones Culturales Argentinas, 1961. Discusses life and works.

VITIER, MEDARDO. "La poesía de Alfonsina Storni." *Revista Nacional de Cultura,* Caracas, year 2, no. 13 (November 1939), pp. 131–148. Original commentary.

WAPNIR, SALOMON. "Alfonsina." Chapter in his *Imágenes y letras.* Buenos Aires: Instituto amigos del libro argentino, 1955. Intelligent, well-researched introductory study.

ZARDOYA, CONCHA. "La muerte en la poesía femenina latinoamericana." *Cuadernos Americanos,* México, year 12, 71, no. 5 (September–October 1953), pp. 233–270. Says some good things, especially in the first pages. Main thrust is to explain her suicide and her love of the sea.

Index

148